Trade and Development
in a Globalized World

Trade and Development in a Globalized World

The Unfair Trade Problem in U.S.-Thai Trade Relations

John M. Rothgeb, Jr., and Benjamas Chinapandhu

LEXINGTON BOOKS

A DIVISION OF
ROWMAN & LITTLEFIELD PUBLISHERS, INC.
Lanham • Boulder • New York • Toronto • Plymouth, UK

LEXINGTON BOOKS

A division of Rowman & Littlefield Publishers, Inc.
A wholly owned subsidiary of The Rowman & Littlefield Publishing Group, Inc.
4501 Forbes Boulevard, Suite 200
Lanham, MD 20706

Estover Road
Plymouth PL6 7PY
United Kingdom

British Library Cataloguing in Publication Information Available

Library of Congress Cataloging-in-Publication Data

Rothgeb, John M.
 Trade and development in a globalized world : the unfair trade problem in U.S.-Thai
trade relations / John M. Rothgeb, Jr. and Benjamas Chinapandhu.
 p. cm.
 Includes bibliographical references and index.
 ISBN-13: 978-0-7391-1655-5 (cloth : alk. paper)
 ISBN-10: 0-7391-1655-X (cloth : alk. paper)
 1. Thailand—Commerce—United States. 2. United States—Commerce—Thailand.
3. Antidumping duties—United States. 4. Dumping (International trade)—Thailand.
I. Benjamas Chinapandhu. II. Title.
 HF3800.55.Z7R67 2007
 382'.709593—dc22   2006023948

Printed in the United States of America

∞™ The paper used in this publication meets the minimum requirements of
American National Standard for Information Sciences—Permanence of Paper for
Printed Library Materials, ANSI/NISO Z39.48-1992.

Contents

CHAPTER ONE

~

Introduction

One of the most important problems in the contemporary international system revolves around developing country access to the advanced country markets that are necessary for promoting economic growth and development. Such access is especially vital in light of the widespread acceptance by many developing states of an exporting for growth strategy that promotes the sale of basic manufactures and other goods in advanced societies as a means for ascending the ladder of economic sophistication. According to this approach, small and poverty-stricken societies are provided with the opportunity to achieve speedier growth than could be sustained by their home markets because they sell their wares in the larger and wealthier markets found in North America, Europe, and other parts of the world.

As more and more developing countries have hopped aboard the exporting for growth bandwagon, their share of world trade has increased. Whereas in 1970 poor countries accounted for approximately 18 percent of exports worldwide, by 1985 that figure had increased to 24 percent, and by 2004 it had reached 33 percent.[1] In the manufacturing arena, by 1998 developing country exports had reached 25 percent of total world exports, which was more than double their 1980 share and nearly three times larger than their 1973 exports.[2] For the most part, these increases in export activity have been in such basic heavy industries as steel and in such light manufactures as textiles, shoes, and selected electronics (televisions, video recorders, etc.).

While the increased economic growth resulting from this export activity has been good news for many developing country corporations and laborers,

1

those same exports have represented threats to the many businesses and workers in advanced societies that must compete with the goods made in poor countries. In response to these increased competitive pressures, those in advanced societies who are affected by developing country exports have sounded a chorus of protectionist demands. These demands, however, have been made in the context of an increasingly open international trading system. The several rounds of GATT (General Agreement on Tariffs and Trade) negotiations held since 1948 have lowered and bound tariffs to such a degree that by the 1980s it was no longer as possible as it once was simply to raise tariffs to bar imports that threatened domestic producers.

The international obligations to maintain open markets that advanced societies have accepted in the post–World War II years have not ended either the calls for protection brought on by developing country exports or the attempts by governments to erect trade barriers. One type of barrier that has become increasingly popular since the mid-1980s relates to unfair trade. Unfair trade involves a situation in which a "producer or its government seeks to manipulate normal market mechanisms to its advantage and to the detriment of" foreign competitors.[3] For more than a century, many governments have maintained laws designed to limit the various practices associated with unfair trade. Among the most prominent of these practices are market manipulations due to dumping and subsidies. Dumping refers to attempts to sell products in export markets at prices that are "less than fair value." As will be seen in chapter 2, less than fair value may be defined in several ways. Subsidies are payments governments provide to domestic producers that enable those producers to sell their goods abroad more easily.

The popularity of trade laws that combat dumping and subsidies is a product of several factors. Among these factors is the ease with which those seeking protection can evoke sympathy from their government and the general public. After all, since dumping and subsidies by definition constitute unfair trade, it is not difficult to convince others that those practices should be resisted and that any loopholes in current laws should be closed as quickly as possible. The analysis found in chapter 2 will illustrate the frequency with which these adjustments have been made over the course of several decades in the antidumping and antisubsidy trade regulations found in the United States, which has been one of the most frequent users of unfair trade restrictions in recent years.

Another reason for the increased use of unfair trade laws is found in their complexity. As governments have rushed to close the just mentioned loopholes, they have created a hodgepodge of exceedingly arcane regulations and procedures that only the best-trained specialists can understand. Because of this complexity, domestic producers in advanced societies have learned over time that merely filing cases against their developing country competitors can saddle those competitors with the costly and confusing burden of defending themselves during what are often lengthy and highly complex investigations. Many trade analysts argue that given the limited financial and technical resources available to many developing country governments and corporations, unfair trade cases frequently so discourage developing country exporters that they abandon export markets.[4] As one scholar maintains, "in some situations the amount of trade does not warrant paying for the attorney and other costs that would be required to defend against an [unfair trade] case, even when a defense would almost certainly prevail."[5] If this happens, then domestic producers are able to blunt the threat from imports even if the case they brought against a foreign competitor is less than solid. Perhaps it is no wonder that one noted trade specialist argues that unfair trade laws have over the past twenty years become the "preferred protectionist devices" for those seeking to restrict imports from developing societies.[6]

An examination of data relating to the use of unfair trade laws reveals just how prominent they now are. One part of the story is found in data from the World Trade Organization (WTO), as presented in tables 1.1 and 1.2. As can be seen in table 1.1, from 1995 to 2002 a total of 2,160 dumping investigations were initiated worldwide, 1,216 of which were aimed at developing country exports. This is 56 percent of the total. One finds a similar picture when examining the actual antidumping (AD) penalties that were applied during the same period, for 723 of the 1,258 measures (57 percent) were placed on developing country exports.

The antisubsidy investigations and duties (known as countervailing duties, or CVDs) between 1995 and 2002 follow much the same pattern. As table 1.2 indicates, 52 percent of the investigations and 57 percent of the penalties were against developing country exports. When considering these figures, it is important to note that between 1995 and 2002 developing societies accounted for an average of 30 percent of world exports.[7] Thus, developing country exports clearly have been targeted for unfair trade complaints and duties far more frequently than their share of world trade would indicate if such complaints were filed evenly against the exports of all societies.

The impact on developing countries of laws restricting dumped and subsidized goods also is demonstrated by data pertaining to the world's two largest export markets, the United States and the European Union (EU). According to Alfred Eckes, a former member of the United States International Trade Commission, in the twenty-three-year period between 1955 and 1978, the United States government investigated 371 dumping complaints. This is

Table 1.1. Antidumping Activity against Developing Countries, 1995–2002

Year	All Countries	Developing Countries	% Against Developing Countries
		Actions Initiated	
1995	157	89	57
1996	224	132	59
1997	243	119	49
1998	255	130	51
1999	355	201	57
2000	288	170	59
2001	362	216	60
2002	276	159	58
Total	2,160	1,216	56
		Duties Imposed	
1995	118	67	57
1996	84	55	65
1997	112	71	63
1998	162	89	55
1999	183	83	45
2000	235	135	57
2001	159	95	60
2002	205	128	62
Total	1,258	723	57

Source: World Trade Organization, AD Initiations by Affected Country and World Trade Organization, AD Measures by Affected Country. Available at www.wto.org.

an average of sixteen complaints per year. By comparison, in the ten-year period from 1979 to 1988 (during which time developing country exports increased significantly) 427 dumping cases were investigated, which is an average of almost 43 cases per year, nearly three times as many cases as in the earlier period.[8] More recently, one finds that between 2000 and 2005 a total of 283 AD and CVD cases were filed in the United States, an average of 47 per year. Of these cases, 171 were against goods from developing countries. This is 60 percent of the total. During the same time period, 124 AD and CVD penalty duties were imposed, 78 of them against developing country products, which is 63 percent of the total.[9] In part, the jump in the filing of dumping cases and in the imposition of dumping duties illustrated by these data is attributable to a change in American law in 1979 (see the discussion in chapter 2). That change, however, was made in response to demands on Congress by American producers who faced foreign competition and wanted a means to protect themselves.

Table 1.2.   Countervailing Activity against Developing Countries, 1995–2002

Year	All Countries	Developing Countries	% Against Developing Countries
		Actions Initiated	
1995	10	3	30
1996	7	2	29
1997	16	9	56
1998	25	9	36
1999	41	23	56
2000	18	15	83
2001	27	16	59
2002	9	2	22
Total	153	79	52
		Duties Imposed	
1995	19	14	74
1996	5	1	20
1997	3	2	67
1998	6	2	33
1999	14	6	43
2000	19	12	63
2001	14	10	71
2002	14	7	50
Total	94	54	57

Source: World Trade Organization, CV Initiations by Affected Country and World Trade Organization, CV Measures by Affected Country. Available at www.wto.org.

As far as the European Union is concerned, data from the European Commission show that between 2000 and 2005, 150 AD and CVD investigations were initiated, which is an average of 25 cases per year. Of these investigations, 105 (70 percent) targeted imports from developing countries. Regarding the imposition of duties, during the same period of time, the EU imposed 126 definitive duty orders, 85 of which were on developing country goods, which is 67 percent of the total.[10] In considering these figures, one should note that between 2001 and 2005 an average of 45 percent of EU imports were from developing countries and that during the same period approximately 38 percent of United States imports came from developing societies.[11] If one juxtaposes these proportions of imports from developing countries with the above figures for the percentages of unfair trade investigations and penalty duties that the EU and the United States apply to goods from developing societies, it becomes apparent that both the EU and the United States target developing country products in a disproportionate way.

When examining the data for the United States and the EU, it is also important to point out that while the United States conducts far more investigations than the EU (283 overall and 171 against developing country products for the United States, as compared to 150 overall and 105 for developing countries for the EU), the imposition of duties is more likely in the EU than in the United States. In the EU, 84 percent of all investigations and 81 percent of those involving developing countries result in a duty, while in the United States 44 percent of all cases and 46 percent of developing country cases lead to a duty. Hence, developing country products are more likely to face investigations in the United States, but may avoid a penalty duty, while in the EU the chance of an investigation is lower, but once an investigation is launched, the probability of a duty is very high.

While the frequency with which their exports have been targeted with unfair trade complaints is a source of irritation in developing societies, the problems caused by these complaints run deeply. For one thing, studies that have examined the specific exports hit by these complaints point out that for the most part the goods in question are usually vital to the growth strategies pursued by developing country governments.[12] Hence, many analysts regard unfair trade complaints as retarding the prospects for economic growth in poor societies, where economic progress is essential to the pursuit of a decent standard of living for the bulk of the people. When one considers the political and social instability that can result from the poverty found in developing countries, and when one contemplates the degree to which international conflict often has its origins in the domestic problems of developing societies, one also can see how important the promotion of economic development is to the maintenance of international stability, especially in a globalized era in which trouble in one region can have rapid and severe repercussions in other parts of the world.[13]

Another problem with unfair trade restrictions is the volume of the exports that are affected by such investigations and duties. To take but one example, it has been estimated that by the mid-1990s approximately 10 percent of Brazil's exports were affected by antidumping duties and another 7 percent were covered by agreements (known as undertakings) that raised prices to avert the imposition of AD penalties.[14] That is, nearly one-fifth of the goods Brazil was exporting were subjected to investigations that limited the ability to do business abroad. Quite naturally, these restrictions were a source of resentment in Brazil and were seen as an attempt by advanced societies to thwart attempts both at economic growth and at the very type of economic competition that capitalism supposedly encourages.

The difficulties the unfair trade rules of many advanced countries pose for their exports have led developing countries to seek relief through the multilateral trade negotiations associated with the GATT and the WTO. Beginning in the Kennedy Round and continuing in the Tokyo and Uruguay Rounds, unfair trade regulations have been on the GATT agenda. During these discussions, developing societies have sought to rein in advanced country unfair trade practices by seeking international regulations pertaining to how and when antidumping and antisubsidy investigations may be conducted and AD and CVD penalties may be imposed. These negotiations, however, have been both controversial and problematic. The controversy stems in part from the passionate belief by those in many advanced countries that dumping and granting subsidies to help exporters create inappropriate advantages that threaten to destroy domestic producers by illegitimate means. Hence, negotiators from advanced societies consistently have fought to retain their unfair trade regulations and to strengthen those laws when it is regarded as necessary to fight what are perceived as new types of dumping and subsidies.[15] Developing country officials have found it difficult to make headway against this opposition, although, as will be seen in chapter 2, some GATT/WTO restrictions have been placed on the way in which unfair trade laws can be used.

Another problem developing countries have faced during multilateral trade negotiations is the exceedingly technical nature of the unfair trade regulations that most countries have on their books. The intricacies associated with unfair trade laws brings a complexity to the discussions during negotiating sessions that makes it extremely difficult for developing country representatives to participate on even terms with advanced country officials. This negotiating handicap is largely attributable to the abovementioned dearth of developing country experts with a sufficient understanding of the nuances of national antidumping and antisubsidy legislation and of the GATT/WTO regulations pertaining to unfair trade.[16]

In response to these needs of developing countries, the WTO has set up technical assistance programs designed to help officials from poorer countries understand international regulations and procedures relating to antidumping and antisubsidy measures. Many observers believe, however, that a lack of technical knowledge continues to hinder the efforts of developing country representatives when they confront the problem of unfair trade.[17] In part, these continuing problems are a product of the absence of a detailed understanding of the precise nature of the barriers and difficulties developing country officials face when it comes to the question of how dumping and subsidy issues should be addressed. If those in developing countries who grapple with the problem of unfair trade are to receive the assistance they need, and if they are to take the proper steps to protect their interests, then an important step along that road must include a careful assessment of exactly what deficiencies they face. One way to begin gathering the information needed for that assessment is to examine in detail the way a specific developing country deals with the problems of unfair trade.

In addition to shedding light on how developing countries may deal more effectively with unfair trade problems, the investigation of the AD and CVD regulations that confront exporters from poor countries may provide insight into the exercise of power in the contemporary international arena. Power involves getting others to do what you want when they do not wish to cooperate. Many analysts argue that the power relationships of the twenty-first century increasingly will be based on new resources. While in the past domination often was a product of the physical capabilities (military forces, control of key raw materials) that actors could bring to bear upon rivals, one might speculate that in the globalized world of the future power may be derived more and more from an actor's control of information and expertise and based on the ability to construct a network of international regulations that enmeshes opponents in a complex structure that renders them unable to respond properly to protect their interests while leaving the actor in question free to operate as it pleases. In other words, information, the interpretation of information, and the ability to dominate rules creating procedures will become a major source of power internationally, just as it already has become in the domestic politics of many countries.

The purpose of this research is to conduct a case study of how governmental officials and private industry representatives from a developing country handle the problems associated with the antidumping and antisubsidy rules and procedures they confront in their largest export market and at the World Trade Organization. By examining such a case, it is expected that insight can be gained into the effects unfair trade regulations have on international development and on power in the current international system. The specific countries examined and the data gathering techniques employed in this research are discussed in the next section.

Research Design

The Case Examined

The developing country that serves as the focal point for the research reported herein is Thailand. Thailand's largest export market is the United

States. Therefore, this analysis involves an in-depth investigation of Thai–United States unfair trade relations. Thailand was selected because it is among the most active international traders in the developing world, its government and industry have reasonably substantial experience in dealing with antidumping and antisubsidy investigations, and it has both a well-organized governmental trade bureaucracy and established private industry groups that deal with trade issues. As illustrated in table 1.3, Thailand exports and imports more goods per capita than does the average country in any of the developing regions around the world. As a result, one might conclude that the Thai government and Thai businesses have above average experience in dealing with trade problems in general. In addition, these figures suggest that trade is important to Thailand and that difficulties relating to trade will command the attention of those responsible for the Thai economy.

Table 1.4 presents data regarding the developing countries that have experienced the most antidumping and antisubsidy (or countervailing) investigations and that have had the most AD and CVD duties applied between 1995 and 2002. As can be seen, Thailand is among the developing world's leaders in each category. Therefore, one can expect Thai government officials and private industry representatives to have an appropriate awareness of the problems that unfair trade investigations and duties can create for developing country exporters.

The organization of the Thai government and of Thai industries (discussed briefly below and more extensively in chapter 3) also is important. Such organization can play a major role in determining how well a country can respond to unfair trade cases, what types of resources it has for participating in international negotiations, and how often it seeks redress for adverse unfair trade decisions either through national courts or by way of the WTO dispute settlement system. A country's ability to engage in each of these activities will in turn affect the degree to which it has experience with

Table 1.3. Imports per capita and Exports per capita for Thailand and Selected Developing Regions, 1999

	Imports	Exports
Thailand	838	973
Latin America	648	579
Sub-Saharan Africa	126	116
East Asia	260	319
South Asia	54	34

Note: All figures are in 1999 U.S. dollars and refer to merchandise imports and exports.
Source: World Bank, World Development Indicators, 2001.

Table 1.4. Developing Countries Most Frequently Targeted for AD and CV Actions and Duties, 1995–2002

AD Cases Initiated	AD Duties Imposed
China (308)	China (212)
South Korea (160)	South Korea (83)
Taiwan (109)	Taiwan (69)
Indonesia (91)	Brazil (51)
India (82)	**Thailand (48)**
Thailand (81)	India (44)
Brazil (68)	Indonesia (39)
South Africa (46)	South Africa (24)
Malaysia (40)	Malaysia (23)
Turkey (30)	Turkey (18)
CV Cases Initiated	CV Duties Imposed
India (32)	India (18)
South Korea (13)	Brazil (8)
Indonesia (8)	Indonesia (5)
Thailand (7)	Argentina (4)
Taiwan (6)	South Korea (4)
Brazil (6)	South Africa (4)
South Africa (6)	Malaysia (3)
Argentina (4)	**Thailand (3)**
Chile (3)	Venezuela (3)

Note: The figures in parentheses refer to the number of cases initiated or duties imposed during the 1995–2002 period.
Source: World Trade Organization, AD Initiations by Affected Country, World Trade Organization, AD Measures by Affected Country, World Trade Organization, CV Initiations by Affected Country, and World Trade Organization, CV Measures by Affected Country. Available at www.wto.org.

many parts of the complex national and international network of unfair trade regulations and procedures.

In light of Thailand's relatively high level of participation in international trade, its experience with unfair trade complaints, and its reasonably extensive trade bureaucracy, one might presume that any problems that Thailand encounters because of AD and CVD actions would also be encountered by other developing countries. This expectation is based on the assumption that a larger than average resource base and a stronger government combine with a greater degree of trading experience to provide Thailand with an ability to handle problems more effectively than can the average developing society. Hence, if Thailand finds itself facing difficulties because of the AD and CVD moves in its largest export market, then one may suspect that those same problems will plague other developing societies. As a result, the examination of the Thai case should provide valuable clues regarding the positions other developing countries find themselves in when it comes to unfair trade.

Data Collection

The data for this case study primarily come from the personal interviews that were conducted with officials from the Thai government and from Thai private industry groups. In some cases, these interviews were supplemented with information from the official documents of the governments of Thailand and the United States. Given the dearth of research based on direct interviews with trade officials from developing countries, the results from the present study should provide an especially valuable picture of precisely how advanced country and WTO unfair trade regulations and procedures affect developing societies.

The initial interviews were conducted in June and July of 2000. Follow-up interviews were held between May and June of 2005 to determine whether there were any changes in the attitudes of the interviewees and whether the problems that were uncovered in 2000 were temporary or of a more permanent nature. The interviews focused on the experiences the respondents have had with AD and CVD cases in the period since the new WTO Antidumping Agreement and the Subsidies and Countervailing Measures Agreement went into effect in 1995. All interviews were conducted in Thai, which is the native language for one of the authors.

The major trade-related agencies in the Thai government were examined because they play the leading role in international negotiations regarding unfair trade, they are the primary respondents in subsidy investigations, and they play an advisory role in dumping cases. The government agencies included in the study were the Bank of Thailand, the Board of Investment, the Bureau of Multilateral Trade Negotiations, and the Bureau of Trade Interests and Remedies. The Bank of Thailand is an independent government agency, the Board of Investment is part of the Office of the Prime Minister, and the Bureau of Multilateral Trade Negotiations and the Bureau of Trade Interests and Remedies are both under the jurisdiction of the Ministry of Commerce. The organization of the Thai government and the specific responsibilities of each of the above agencies is described in more detail in chapter 3.

In addition to the above government agencies, two industries were studied. These were the canned pineapple industry and the steel industry. These industries were selected because they are prominent exporters and because they have been the targets of several American dumping and subsidy complaints. As will be explored in more detail in chapter 3, examining these industries also allows for one to compare the attitudes and perceptions found in an industry (steel) that has faced a relatively large number of AD and CVD complaints with views from an industry that has been the object of far fewer unfair trade investigations. Exploring private industry representatives is vital to a complete understanding of how developing countries handle unfair trade cases because private corporations are the primary respondents in dumping investigations. Private companies also frequently have a part in setting the government's agendas for international negotiations and for new trade legislation.

In exploring the canned pineapple and steel industries, the Thai Pineapple Packers' Group, the Thai Food Processors' Association, the Thai Iron and Steel Industry Club, the Federation of Thai Industries, and the Joint WTO Committee on Commerce, Industry, and Banking in Thailand were examined. The Joint WTO Committee is an organization that includes as members the Board of Trade, the Federation of Thai Industries, and the Thai Bankers' Association. Among the members of the Federation of Thai Industries are the Thai Pineapple Packers' Group, the Thai Food Processors' Association, and the Thai Iron and Steel Industry Club. Each of these industry organizations is discussed more completely in chapter 3.

Nine clusters of variables served as the focal point for the interviews that were conducted. These variable clusters were selected to provide an in-depth view of the types of problems the Thai government and Thai industries face, how they seek to solve these problems, and whether assistance is available to Thailand from American sources or from the WTO. The specific questions included in each variable cluster are in Appendix B. The nine clusters of variables are:

Knowledge Problems: This category examines how well equipped Thai officials are to understand the intricacies of American and WTO rules regarding dumping and subsidy issues.

Procedural Issues: These questions explore the way in which Thai subjects perceive and react to the mechanisms the United States employs when conducting unfair trade investigations.

Cooperation: This category investigates the degree to which Thai respondents assist United States government agencies when they conduct unfair trade investigations.

Assistance: This group of questions looks at whether Thai industries facing unfair trade actions can obtain aid from the Thai government, the United States government, or the WTO when they respond to the investigations.

Burden: These questions pertain to the costs Thai respondents incur when responding to unfair trade actions.

Settlement: This category explores the types of concessions Thai respondents make in order to terminate the unfair trade cases they confront.

Retaliation and Appeal: These questions examine whether Thai officials either seek to counter United States unfair trade actions or seek redress for any grievances they may have through the use of the United States court system or by employing the WTO dispute settlement system.

Negotiating Process: These questions explore the degree to which Thai officials are interested in pushing for new international discussions to change or modify existing WTO agreements regarding unfair trade.

Impact Issues: This group of questions examines how the government and private industry in Thailand has changed, or is considering changing, the way they handle development policy in response to unfair trade problems.

Through the examination of the above categories of variables it should be possible to develop a relatively complete picture of the difficulties Thai officials confront when dealing with unfair trade cases and how those officials seek to handle those problems. Information relating to the general needs of developing countries also should be uncovered by examining these issues.

Chapter Outline

The coming pages are divided into three additional chapters. The next chapter examines the evolution of United States antidumping and countervailing duty laws from the time they were first developed in the late nineteenth and early twentieth centuries until the present. The original purposes of these laws are examined, as is the manner in which they have changed over time to encompass new objectives and to play a new role in protecting American firms from foreign competition. In addition, this chapter considers how the GATT and the WTO have affected American unfair trade regulations. This examination of United States and WTO regulations and procedures is designed to acquaint the reader with the major issues and problems associated with unfair trade and will set the stage for the later analysis.

Chapter 3 investigates the problems Thailand confronts when handling unfair trade cases. It begins by describing the role Thailand plays in international commerce and as an American trading partner. Following this, the key Thai government agencies that handle unfair trade matters and the private industry organizations mentioned above are discussed. The results of the interviews with key Thai government officials and private industry representatives are then reported and analyzed.

The final chapter considers the policy recommendations one can derive from the research results and what the research has to say about promoting international development. The policy recommendations are divided into sections relating to domestic reforms in Thailand and other developing countries, changes at the World Trade Organization that might better suit the needs of developing societies, how developing actors might alter the strategies they use when pursuing their trade-related interests in the United States, and the tactics developing countries might employ to ensure that they gain more from international trade negotiations. In discussing international development, the focus is on what the results imply for the exercise of power, for protectionism, and for international interdependence in the current global system.

In addition to these chapters, two appendixes are included. Appendix A provides definitions and explanations for the terminology and abbreviations found throughout the book. Appendix B includes a complete list of the questions employed during the interviews.

Notes

1. These trade figures are based on calculations made from data in U.N., *Yearbook of International Trade Statistics*, various years and from United Nations Conference on Trade and Development (UNCTAD), *UNCTAD Handbook of Statistics*, 2005, p. 14.

2. Peter Gallagher, *Guide to the WTO and Developing Countries*, London: Kluwer Law International, 2000, p. 7.

3. John M. Rothgeb, Jr., *U.S. Trade Policy: Balancing Economic Dreams and Political Realities*, Washington, DC: CQ Press, 2001, p. 95.

4. Asoke Mukerji, "Developing Countries and the WTO: Issues of Implementation," *Journal of World Trade*, vol. 34, no. 6, 2000, p. 69; Anne Krueger, "The Developing Countries and the Next Round of Multilateral Trade Negotiations," *The World Economy*, vol. 22, no. 7, September 1999, p. 913; Constantine Michalopoulos, "The Developing Countries in the WTO," *The World Economy*, vol. 22, no. 1, January 1999, pp. 136–37.

5. John H. Jackson, *The World Trading System: Law and Policy of International Economic Relations*, Cambridge, MA: MIT Press, 1997, p. 271.

6. T. N. Srinisasan, "Developing Countries in the World Trading System: From GATT, 1947, to the Third Ministerial Meeting of the WTO, 1999," *The World Economy*, vol. 22, no. 8, November 1999, p. 1062.

7. This average is based on data from UNCTAD, *UNCTAD Handbook of Statistics*, 2005, p. 14.

8. Alfred E. Eckes, "Antidumping after the Uruguay Round: A Former Administrator's Perspective," in *International Commercial Policy: Issues for the 1990s*, ed. Mordechai E. Kreinin, Washington, DC: Taylor and Francis, 1993, pp. 30–31.

9. The data for the years 2000–2005 are from United States International Trade Commission, "Import Injury Investigations Case Statistics, FY 1980–2004," October 2005, available at www.usitc.gov.

10. These data are from European Commission, "Anti-Dumping and Anti-Subsidy Statistics Covering the Year," available at http://ee.europa.eu/comm/trade.

11. The data for the United States are from U.S. International Trade Administration, "National Trade Data," available at www.usita.gov. The data for the European Union are from European Commission, "Trade Issues: Bilateral Trade Relations," May 22, 2006.

12. Krueger, "Developing Countries and the Next Round," p. 94; Julio Nogues, "The Cost to Latin America of Adopting Unfair Trade Policies," in *International Commercial Policy: Issues for the 1990s*, ed. Mordechai E. Kreinin, Washington, DC: Taylor and Francis, 1993, p. 41.

13. For discussions of domestic and international conflict in developing countries, see John M. Rothgeb, Jr., *Defining Power: Influence and Force in the Contemporary International System*, New York: St. Martin's Press, 1993, pp. 75–76 and John M. Rothgeb, Jr., *Foreign Investment and Political Conflict in Developing Countries*, Westport, CT: Praeger Publishers, 1996, pp. 1–3.

14. Nogues, "The Cost to Latin America," p. 42.

15. David Palmeter, "A Commentary on the WTO Antidumping Code," *Journal of World Trade*, vol. 30, no. 4, August 1996, pp. 67–68.

16. Michalopoulos, "The Developing Countries in the WTO," p. 127.

17. Ibid., p. 138.

CHAPTER TWO

~

The Evolution of United States Antidumping and Countervailing Duty Rules and Procedures

The purpose of this chapter is to examine United States unfair trade rules and procedures. To review the discussion in the introduction, unfair trade involves "a situation in which a foreign producer or its government seeks to manipulate normal market mechanisms to its advantage and to the detriment" of competitors in another society.[1] Two of the most common forms of unfair trade involve grants of subsidies by a government to its exporting industries and dumping. As will be discussed below, dumping constitutes the sale of exports at prices that are "less than fair value" (sometimes also referred to as "normal value"), which can be defined and calculated in several ways. For decades, the United States Congress and the General Agreement on Tariffs and Trade (GATT) have regarded foreign subsidies and dumping as potential threats to domestic industries that must compete with imports. This is because both of these activities allow imports to be priced at such artificially low levels that they may undercut the prices charged by domestic producers and harm domestic businesses and/or drive them into bankruptcy.

Under GATT and World Trade Organization (WTO) rules dating to the late 1940s and according to American trade laws from the early part of the twentieth century, unfair trade practices can be countered by remedies that may be imposed by a government to protect its domestic producers. For the most part, these remedies involve the imposition of import duties to offset the benefits resulting from the unfair trading. In the case of dumping, the duty is an antidumping (AD) charge. When subsidies are involved, the penalty imposed is referred to as a countervailing duty (CVD).

When examining the international trading problems of developing countries, one finds that there are significant difficulties relating to the rules advanced countries use when deciding to impose AD and CVD measures. As the largest of the advanced countries, the controversies relating to AD and CVD rules are especially prominent in the trading relationships the United States has with poorer societies. In part, these controversies are a product of the complexity of American law. Another factor leading to trouble is the fact that United States AD and CVD practices have evolved considerably in the decades since they were first created and now can be used in ways that go beyond the original purposes the laws were passed to serve. Indeed, many analysts argue that American unfair trade laws have changed so greatly over the years that they are now little more than convenient devices that may be used to shield domestic producers from foreign competition, both fair and unfair.

The disputes regarding unfair trade extend beyond the rules advanced countries use to handle dumping and subsidies and touch as well on the WTO. This is because the WTO and its predecessor, the GATT, contains regulations that permit countries to impose unfair trade penalties while at the same time limiting the circumstances under which those penalties may be employed. For the most part, during the negotiations relating to the creation and modification of these international unfair trade rules, the United States has focused on ensuring that it retains a relatively free hand in imposing unfair trade duties, while most developing countries have sought to restrict the conditions under which such penalties may be employed. As a result, the WTO and GATT negotiations relating to unfair trade have been the scene for many disagreements between the United States and developing societies.

In order to provide a proper foundation for understanding the problems Thailand faces regarding American AD and CVD practices, it is therefore necessary to describe carefully both United States AD and CVD rules and procedures and to consider how they have been affected by the agreements that established the WTO. To that end, this chapter considers how and why American AD and CVD regulations were first set up and how they have evolved over time. With this information in hand, it will then be possible to focus in a later chapter on the Thai experience with American unfair trade laws and on what this implies for developing countries in general.

The analysis in this chapter begins by considering the motivations behind the legislation that first established United States AD laws and the manner in which those laws have changed over time. To this end, the logic behind the major American AD laws is described, as is their content. Following this, the motivations for the early CVD laws are described and the evolution of CVD legislation is considered. To facilitate the discussion, the chapter is divided into two sections, with the first looking at AD laws and the second at legislation regarding CVDs.

Antidumping in the United States

In its earliest manifestations, antidumping legislation in the United States was closely associated with the American antitrust movement. The earliest American AD laws therefore were patterned on the approach used in antitrust legislation. As time passed, however, intense pressure built to adjust United States AD laws because they were seen as too cumbersome and as inadequate to the task at hand, which was to halt foreign attempts to flood the United States with inappropriately priced goods. After World War II, two additional factors influencing AD legislation had to do with the constant lowering of American tariffs and the international trade agreements entered into by the United States first as a party to the GATT and later as a member of the WTO. Each of these factors is described below and their effects on American AD laws are discussed.

Antitrust and Antidumping

One of the primary motivations for the world's first antidumping laws can be found in the antitrust and antimonopoly movements found in many advanced countries in the late nineteenth and early twentieth centuries. The antitrust activities of the time were largely predicated on the notion that as market economies matured one often found a considerable degree of consolidation among businesses as larger firms either bought their smaller competitors or forced them into bankruptcy. For many, this consolidation brought with it the threat that if firms became so large that they could dominate the production and sale of specific goods, then they would be in a position to force consumers to pay ever-higher prices for those goods. As a result, many analysts concluded that regulations were needed to ensure that markets would remain competitive.

In the United States, the first antitrust law was the Sherman Act of 1890. According to this law, "every contract, combination . . . or conspiracy in restraint of trade" was forbidden.[2] Subsequent enforcement of this law treated predatory pricing as one type of evidence indicating that there was a conspiracy to restrain trade. Predatory pricing was defined as selling goods at an abnormally low level in order to harm one's competitors. Evidence that a sale involved predatory pricing was found in such practices as selling below the cost of production and selling the same good for different prices in varying parts of the United States.[3]

Congress passed additional antitrust legislation in 1914 when it set up the Federal Trade Commission (FTC) and enacted the Clayton Act. Among other things, the FTC was designed to prevent "unfair methods of competition" in interstate commerce, while Section 2 of the Clayton Act was aimed at predatory pricing. In Section 2, Congress made it illegal to vary the prices different customers were charged for the same type of goods if the price differences were designed to reduce competition and to set up monopolies.[4]

The concern with protecting against monopolies and the predatory pricing that firms used to destroy competitors was not restricted to the domestic market. By the early 1900s, American businesses increasingly claimed that they faced circumstances in which foreign producers were using monopoly-like tactics when they sold goods in the United States market. In particular, British and German companies were accused of selling goods in the United States for prices that were so artificially low that American firms were unable to compete.[5] When federal courts ruled that the Sherman Act did not apply to imports because American laws could not be presumed to have extraterritorial reach, the stage was set for the first antidumping legislation in the United States.[6]

The first American attack on foreign monopolies came in the Wilson Tariff of 1894. Section 73 of that tariff made it a criminal offense for individuals or corporations to use imports to restrain trade within the United States. As a device for preventing dumping, this law proved ineffective. One reason is explained in a Congressional Budget Office study, for "normally . . . only the exporter—not the importer—is involved with predatory intent, and the exporter's behavior occurs outside the United States," thus raising the issue of extraterritoriality. Another difficulty related to proving that foreigners intended to restrain sales in the United States.[7]

The next attack on foreign monopolies came in 1916 and involved a change in legal tactics. The Antidumping Act of 1916 was in part a response to complaints from United States manufacturers that many German enterprises were responding to World War I by banding together into cartels and were exporting such goods as steel and chemicals to the United States at predatory prices. Substantial pressures were placed on President Woodrow Wilson to raise the American tariff to shield domestic producers from such behavior. Instead of agreeing to a tariff increase, Wilson recommended that Congress enact legislation to prevent the sale in the United States of foreign-made goods that were offered at "prices substantially less than the market value in the principal markets of the country producing the exports."[8] In effect, this law took aim at foreign monopolistic practices by focusing on the predatory pricing tactics that trusts and cartels so often used to destroy their competitors. Criminal and civil penalties were established to discourage and prevent the prohibited behavior.[9]

As it happened, the Antidumping Act of 1916 fell short of its central purpose. As was the case with the Wilson Tariff, it was difficult to establish intent and to prove that there was a conspiracy to harm American producers. Moreover, since the law provided for criminal penalties, the standards of evidence were so high that no successful complaint was ever filed under the law.[10]

Antidumping in the Interwar Years

The problems associated with the 1916 law led Congress in 1919 to direct the Tariff Commission to review the question of dumping and to recommend appropriate remedies. In its report, the Tariff Commission noted the difficulties associated with proving intent and stated that an administrative procedure for handling dumping might prove more effective than the judicial approach employed in the legislation from 1916.[11]

To redress the difficulties pointed out by the Tariff Commission, Congress passed the Antidumping Act of 1921 as a part of the Emergency Tariff Act that was enacted that same year. This law became the basic guidepost for United States antidumping procedures until 1979. Under the 1921 law, four principles were set up as the foundation for the American approach to dumping. The first principle established antidumping duties on foreign goods as the means for handling the problem of dumping. This replaced the civil damages and criminal fines that had been at the heart of the 1916 law. A second principle eliminated the need to demonstrate both predatory intent and that foreigners meant to destroy or harm an American producer. Instead, Congress specified that an injury or the likelihood of an injury would be sufficient for imposing antidumping duties. Third, the determination of when antidumping duties should be imposed became an administrative decision that was placed in the hands of the Treasury Department, which was given broad discretionary authority over the matter. American courts no longer would play a role in the initial decision making about dumping.[12]

Finally, a new procedure was created for evaluating whether dumping had occurred. Normally, dumping was determined through a comparison of the price charged in the United States and in the home market of the corporation that produced the good. If the American price was lower, then it was assumed that there was dumping. On occasion, however, there were insufficient sales in the home market. To handle such a circumstance, the 1921 law permitted the Treasury Department to construct the cost of production (referred to today as "constructed value").[13] The constructed value would be the sum of the cost of the materials used in producing the good, the packing charges incurred in preparing the good for export, the cost of transporting the good to its ultimate sales destination, and an appropriate profit margin.[14] This constructed value would then serve as the basis for the price comparisons used to determine if there was dumping.

These four principles resulted in a transformation in the way the United States handled dumping. Using antidumping duties to address the problem meant that the focus shifted from penalizing foreigners through fines and criminal prosecution to punishing them by restricting their ability to sell goods in the American market. The use of an injury standard eliminated the need to establish predatory intent. Making the decision about the imposition of duties administrative lowered the standards of evidence that were required. And finally, allowing for a constructed value made it far more difficult for foreigners to evade dumping determinations by refusing to cooperate with American investigators by providing them with pricing information.

Modifications of the 1921 law came in 1922 and 1930. In the Tariff Act of 1922 (known as the Fordney-McCumber Tariff), Congress limited judicial reviews of Treasury Department antidumping decisions to interpretations of the law and eliminated the responsibility of courts for examining administrative decisions and procedures. In addition, the Tariff Commission was assigned the task of making injury determinations.[15] The 1930 revision was included in the Tariff Act of 1930 (the Smoot-Hawley Tariff). This law adopted the four principles for antidumping found in the Antidumping Act of 1921, elaborated on the definition of unfair trade to include not only harming their ability to do business, but also impairing the efficiency of American producers, and facilitated the imposition and collection of duties whenever the Treasury Department determined that dumping had occurred.[16]

Hence, in the years between World War I and World War II, the American approach to dumping changed considerably from what it had been in 1916. The laws passed in 1921, 1922, and 1930 took decision making away from United States courts and placed it in the hands of a bureaucratic agency where it could be subject to far greater domestic political pressures. At the same time, it became both much easier for American producers to secure favorable findings when they alleged that they were victims of dumping and more difficult for foreign corporations to challenge American dumping decisions. The elimination of the need to demonstrate an intent to harm American businesses also began shifting the logic behind the prohibition of dumping. Previously, the focus was on the predatory pricing tactic that is associated with the attempt to establish a monopoly. In the new laws, the central antidumping justification was built around the idea that foreign pricing practices in themselves should not be permitted to damage American firms even if there was no evidence that these practices were part of a monopolistic strategy.

Post-War Antidumping

In the years after World War II, the trade agreements negotiated by the United States under the Reciprocal Trade Agreements program and as a part of the GATT began the process of lowering American tariffs on a continuing basis.[17] The high tariffs of the interwar years that had shielded American businesses from foreign competition increasingly were a thing of the past. As a result, American producers began looking for alternatives to provide themselves with a means for avoiding international competitive pressures. One such alternative was to expand the reach of antidumping legislation. Therefore, pressures built in Congress that called for revisions that would make antidumping laws fit the new needs of American corporations.

One response to the demands for new approaches to antidumping came in 1954 when Congress passed the Customs Simplification Act. Under this law, a three-month time limit for determining whether imports were selling for less than fair value (that is, were being dumped) was placed on the Treasury Department.[18] This was meant to eliminate the lengthy delays that many American corporations claimed accompanied Treasury Department investigations.

A second response came in 1958 when the Tariff Act of 1930, which was (and is) still in effect, was amended in several ways. First, it was required that tie votes by the Tariff Commission regarding injury due to dumping would be recorded in favor of the American complainant, thus facilitating affirmative dumping findings. Next, it was specified that dumping price comparisons need not be based on identical merchandise. Instead, the Treasury Department was permitted to compare sales prices in the United States and in other markets of goods that were merely similar, while making appropriate adjustments for the fact that the goods were not identical. Finally, a third method for making price comparisons was set up. As may be recalled, in 1921 two types of comparison were created, one based on the examination of sales in the United States and sales in the home market and the other on the use of constructed values. The new type of comparison allowed for the examination of sales in third country markets when sales in the home market were negligible. According to this method, if American prices were lower than the prices charged in the third country export market, then dumping in the United States would be presumed.[19]

The most sweeping of the post-war changes in antidumping laws came in the Trade Act of 1974 and the Trade Agreements Act of 1979. The Trade Act of 1974 was the legislation that permitted the president to participate in the Tokyo Round of GATT talks. When considering this major new trade bill, Congress took the opportunity to change two key features of American antidumping rules. The first change set strict time limits on foreign firms for filling out the complex questionnaires used in dumping investigations and tightened the time limits under which the Treasury Department could conduct its dumping investigations. These alterations increased the problems foreign firms confronted when they faced dumping allegations and encouraged American firms to use dumping complaints to harass their foreign competitors.[20]

The second change altered the definition of dumping to include any sales below the cost of production, even if the selling prices in the home country market and in the United States were the same. Moreover, technical changes were made in the methods used for calculating dumping that allowed American investigators to exclude from consideration sales in the home market (or in third markets when they were used as a basis for comparison) at prices below the average cost of production for a specified period of time. This change greatly enhanced the probability that an American dumping investigation would lead to a determination that dumping had occurred.[21]

The provisions found in the Trade Agreements Act of 1979 also were designed to assist American businesses seeking protection. This law was enacted to finalize the agreements reached during the Tokyo Round (1973–1979) between the United States and the other parties to the GATT. One part of the 1979 legislation wrote into law provisions pertaining to the GATT Antidumping Code that was set up during the Tokyo Round. The new GATT code, which was voluntary, replaced the GATT Antidumping Code (also voluntary) created during the Kennedy Round (1964–1967). An important component of the new Code was the requirement that dumping duties only could be imposed if a country determined not only that foreign goods were dumped, but also that the act of dumping had injured a domestic industry. Thus, the 1979 law amended the Tariff Act of 1930 to implement the Tokyo Round Code. As the reader may recall, the earlier laws had allowed for positive dumping findings if there was a threat of injury or if dumping impaired the efficiency of American businesses. Under the new law, one was required to demonstrate actual injury.[22] Hence, this part of the new law made it somewhat more difficult to obtain a positive dumping ruling.

A second major provision in the 1979 law, however, clearly was designed to help American firms. This provision shifted the authority for conducting dumping investigations from the Treasury Department to the Commerce Department's International Trade Administration (ITA). In doing this, Congress was replacing the internationalist and free trade–oriented Treasury Department with a Commerce Department that was more sympathetic to American businesses and more likely to take a protectionist stance. It was expected in Congress that this move would result in more frequent findings that would favor United States companies.[23]

A third provision in 1979 related to annual reviews of all dumping decisions to determine that antidumping duties were maintained at a proper level and to ensure that agreements that suspended investigations were still appropriate. Suspension agreements were sometimes employed as an alternative to AD duties. Such agreements usually called for foreigners to raise the prices of their exports to levels that eliminated the possibility of dumping. The new law also allowed for a judicial review of antidumping decisions that did not favor American complainants. These moves clearly were intended to maintain the pressure on foreign firms by constantly examining and reexamining their pricing practices. In addition, allowing for a judicial review was meant to give American firms yet another recourse if they were not satisfied with the outcome of a dumping investigation.[24]

The final major dumping-oriented feature of the 1979 law had to do with the data employed when developing constructed values. One problem that consistently had bedeviled dumping investigations pertained to the acquisition of the data needed to develop comparative pricing values when sales in the home market or in other export markets were inadequate for that purpose. Under the new law, a procedure labeled "best information available" (BIA) was devised that authorized the ITA to seek out the highest quality data it could obtain whenever it confronted a shortage of information relating to foreign pricing practices or to foreign costs of production. In many cases, this meant that in practice the data would be provided by the American corporation that was filing the dumping complaint.[25] Hence, BIA became yet another legal provision that slanted dumping investigations in favor of American businesses. BIA also came to serve as a powerful lever for forcing foreign firms to cooperate with ITA investigations since a refusal to do so invariably led to the use of BIA and to the imposition of higher AD rates.

The fifth post-war adjustment in American dumping policy came in the Trade and Tariff Act of 1984. This law responded in part to industry complaints that arose during a recession that struck the United States in 1981 and 1982. During this recession, several American industries argued that they were under assault from foreign competition and that dumping tactics were being employed by their international competitors. Steel and textile producers were especially vocal in this regard. These businesses demanded that Congress change American antidumping laws to prevent foreigners from continuing their unwarranted behavior.[26]

Congress responded to these pressures by including section 612 in the new trade bill it was devising in 1984. Section 612 clarified the circumstances under which the International Trade Commission (ITC) could resort to cumulation when making injury determinations in AD cases. The use of cumulation meant that during injury investigations the ITC would not focus solely on the damage done by the dumped goods from a single foreign source, but would consider the total effect of all dumped imports of like products. Using this approach greatly increased the probability of a positive injury determination even when the dumping involved in any particular case was so small that it could not plausibly be regarded as injuring American producers. Prior to 1984, ITC decisions about whether to cumulate were made on a case-by-case basis, and dumping by smaller foreign firms often was not seen as harming their competitors in the United States. Section 612 eliminated ITC discretion in this matter by setting three standards for using cumulation: (1) the products in question compete with American made goods and with other imports, (2) the goods must be marketed during the same time period, and (3) the goods must be under an AD investigation.[27] These rules meant that cumulation henceforth would be a more widely employed practice, that smaller foreign firms (including many from developing countries) would be more likely to face positive injury determinations, and that American producers would have an incentive to file more cases against foreign firms, both large and small. Not only did this change ease the standard needed for positive dumping determinations, but it also was another legal provision that encouraged American firms to use dumping cases as a means for harassing foreign competitors.

A second provision in the 1984 law, found in section 609, granted the ITA the authority to initiate dumping investigations when there was "persistent injurious dumping" from more than one country.[28] This meant that the ITA was expected to be especially vigilant if more than one AD order was in effect, which in turn tempted American producers to file cases to create the conditions under which ITA self-initiation would be required. In addition, section 221 of the law established the Trade Remedy Assistance Center within the Commerce Department to provide American businesses with information and assistance regarding antidumping procedures and investigations. Beyond this, the law also instructed all American trade-related agencies, such as the Office of the United States Trade Representative (USTR), the ITC, and the ITA, to give technical assistance to American firms as they prepared their antidumping petitions.[29]

The provisions of the 1984 law, however, did not all move in the direction of facilitating the use of dumping as a protective device. In one important respect, this law made it more difficult to obtain a favorable ruling. This part of the law was found in the provision in section 620 that changed the dumping calculation methodology used by the ITA. Prior to 1984, it was possible for the ITA to compare individual prices over a period of time in the United States market with the average foreign price for the same period of time. If the American price fluctuated during that time period, then positive dumping determinations could result, even if the average American price for the period would not support such a finding. In addition, the ITA usually omitted United States sales prices that were above the average foreign price when making dumping calculations. This also increased the chance of a positive determination. The new calculation methodology for the most part permitted the average United States price to be compared to the average foreign price, thus reducing the probability of positive determinations due to price fluctuations.[30] This change in calculation methodology was in part a product of foreign pressure and of the American desire to offer foreign critics of American antidumping practices an incentive to participate in a new round of GATT negotiations.

The next set of changes in American antidumping rules were included in the Omnibus Trade and Competitiveness Act (OTCA) of 1988. This law amended the Tariff Act of 1930 to bring two foreign practices that were plaguing American firms within the scope of United States law. The first was referred to as circumvention, and the second was third country dumping. Circumvention, which the Smith Corona Corporation took the lead in raising as an issue, involved a circumstance in which foreign producers attempted to side-step American antidumping rules through such tactics as shipping slightly changed or somewhat updated products or by sending parts to the United States or to a third country for final assembly into finished goods. To counter these practices, the OTCA authorized the Commerce Department to extend an AD order to cover any of the just mentioned forms of behavior.[31] This was known as a grant of anticircumvention authority.

The third country dumping issue was raised primarily by the American semiconductor industry, which felt that it was confronting devastating and unfair competition from Japanese firms that dumped both in the United States and in third country markets. Semiconductor firms asserted that these Japanese tactics were depriving them of both American and foreign markets, and that the traditional American approach to antidumping would do little to reverse the situation unless it was amended to include third country dumping.[32]

In an attempt to counter third country dumping, the OTCA included in section 1318 a directive to the USTR that when necessary requests should be made for third countries to initiate antidumping actions as a counter for behavior that was injuring American firms. Article 12 of the Tokyo Round Antidumping Code included provisions that permitted requests of this sort. Section 1318 further specified that if a third country refused to comply with an American request for an antidumping investigation, then the USTR should consult with the affected American corporations to find an alternative remedy.[33] As it happened, few third countries responded favorably to these American requests unless they had domestic industries of their own that were damaged.

Recent Antidumping Legislation

The most recent antidumping legislation in the United States has taken two forms. The first is embodied in the law that was passed to implement the results of the Uruguay Round of GATT negotiations and to make the United States a member of the World Trade Organization. The second is found in what is known as the Byrd Amendment.

Beginning with the former, the changes in American antidumping rules stemming from the Uruguay Round are found in the Uruguay Round Agreements Act (URAA), which was passed in December 1994 and took effect on January 1, 1995. During the Uruguay Round, one of the most contentious issues discussed had to do with dumping. Many countries, especially developing countries, raised the issue because they felt that American laws unreasonably restricted their ability to sell in the American market.[34] For its part, the United States was determined to maintain its antidumping laws because many American producers and members of Congress regarded these laws as an essential tool for combating unfair trade. As a result, lengthy debates took place that eventually produced a compromise Antidumping Agreement that differed from its Tokyo and Kennedy Round counterparts in that it was required of all WTO members, while the earlier codes had been voluntary.

The URAA amended Title VII of the Tariff Act of 1930 to introduce four major changes to American antidumping rules. These changes are found in the Tariff Act of 1930, as amended. The URAA also included one additional change that did not touch on any of the provisions found in the 1930 law or in any of its amended versions. Before turning to the discussion of the amendments to the 1930 law, it is important to note that the URAA reaffirmed the three-part method previously employed to determine if a product was dumped. Sections 223 and 224 slightly altered sections 772 and 773 of the 1930 law to state that the preferred method for calculating dumping should be a comparison of the American sales price with the country of origin sales price. As was discussed earlier, when such a comparison is not possible, then two other methods may be used. One compares the price in the United States to the price in another export market, while the other employs a constructed value which is compared to the sale price in the United States.[35]

The first amendment to the 1930 law pertained to what is known as "de minimis" dumping margins. De minimis refers to the price difference that is allowed to terminate an antidumping investigation. Prior to the URAA, American law set this at less than 0.5 percent. That is, if a dumping margin was equal to or greater than 0.5 percent, then an appropriate AD duty was imposed. If the margin was less than 0.5 percent, then it was referred to as a de minimis case and treated as having a zero margin, and AD duties were not imposed. During the Uruguay Round negotiations, the United States agreed to revise this standard upward and a less than 2 percent de minimis was established for dumping investigations.[36] This de minimis change was a product of an American concession to developing countries.

The second amendment to the 1930 law had to do with the question of third country dumping. As was discussed above, by the late 1980s, several American companies had developed concerns about foreign, especially Japanese, dumping in markets that previously had absorbed large quantities of American exports. When the initial United States attempt to deal with this problem in the Omnibus Trade and Competitiveness Act of 1988 proved less than satisfactory, the issue was included in the Uruguay Round talks.

These negotiations led to Article 14 of the WTO Antidumping Agreement, which permits a country to conduct an antidumping investigation at the request of another country. This provision did not give the United States all that it wanted, however, for the decision as to whether a country would actually conduct the requested investigation was made voluntary. Article 14 of the WTO AD Agreement was incorporated into section 783 of the 1930 law. Section 783 set up procedures by which the United States would respond to requests from other countries that the United States conduct dumping investigations.[37]

The third amendment to the 1930 law pertained to cumulation. Under previous American cumulation rules, an injury determination in an antidumping case could be positive if it was found that dumping had occurred and that the total effects of all of the dumped imports of the goods in question were harming an American industry. The new Uruguay Round cumulation rules specified that cumulation would not be applied if a country met the de minimis standard and the imports from that country accounted for less than 3 percent of the total imports of a particular product. An exception to this new rule can be made if the total imports from all countries that individually have less that 3 percent of American imports collectively account for 7 percent or more of total imports. These provisions are in sections 771 (24) of the 1930 law and in section 222(e) of the URAA.[38]

The fourth amendment to the 1930 law found in the URAA set procedures for reviewing AD duties. Section 751 of the 1930 law was changed to bring it into conformity with Articles 11:2 and 11:3 of the WTO Antidumping Agreement. Under article 11:2 those subject to AD duties may request a review to determine "whether the continued imposition of the duty is necessary to offset dumping." If the review indicates that dumping has ceased and that injuries to American producers have stopped, then the AD duties are ended. Article 11:3 pertains to "sunset reviews," which are required within five years after AD duties are first imposed. If during the sunset review the Commerce Department concludes that dumping has stopped and that it would not resume in the absence of duties, and if the ITC determines that the elimination of AD duties would not lead to future injury for American producers, then the AD duties are abolished.[39] Prior to the setting of these time limits, American antidumping rules made no arrangements for terminating antidumping duties once they were in place.

The final major change in American antidumping rules to emerge from the Uruguay Round is contained in section 129 of the URAA. Section 129 sets the procedures by which the United States responds to WTO dispute settlement panels that rule that an American antidumping decision does not conform to the WTO Antidumping Agreement. According to section 129, whenever a WTO panel rules against the United States, the USTR may request that the ITC and/or the Department of Commerce issue a report regarding the steps needed to bring the United States into conformity with WTO rules. Once this report is issued, the USTR is then directed to consult with the House Ways and Means Committee and the Senate Appropriations Committee. Following this, the USTR may direct the Department of Commerce to terminate the inappropriate antidumping dumping. The president is authorized, however, to overrule or modify this termination after consulting with the Ways and Means and Appropriations Committees.[40]

In general, a review of the Uruguay Round Antidumping Agreement reveals that for the most part it set new limits on American antidumping rules. These new limits are found in the de minimis standards, the restrictions on the use of cumulation in injury determinations, the sunset review, and the requirements relating to the WTO dispute settlement system. The only area that extended the reach of American AD rules pertained to third country dumping. But the potential benefits in this area were muted by the fact that the decisions relating to the initiation of third country investigations are voluntary.

On additional recent change in American antidumping legislation is found in the Byrd Amendment. The Byrd Amendment, named for Senator Robert Byrd (D, W.V.), is formally known as the Continued Dumping and Subsidy Offset Act, which is a part of Title X of the Agricultural and Related Agencies Appropriations Act of 2000. Title X amends Title VII of the Tariff Act of 1930 by inserting a new section 754. Under the terms of this amendment, the proceeds from the collection of antidumping duties are no longer paid into the United States treasury, as had been previous practice. Instead, these funds are slated for annual distribution to the American producers affected by the dumping behavior of foreign firms. Section 754 defines a producer as a "manufacturer, producer, farmer, rancher, or worker" that was party to the antidumping petition and that continues to produce the product covered by the antidumping duties. Parties that have ceased production are not eligible for the distribution of funds.[41] As of early 2003, the U.S. government had paid out over $550 million in accordance with the terms of the Byrd Amendment.[42]

While the Byrd Amendment is popular among Americans who compete with exports because it adds an additional disincentive to discourage foreign companies from dumping, it has proven extremely controversial abroad. Within two months after its passage in October 2000, nine WTO members (Australia, Brazil, Chile, the European Union, India, Indonesia, Japan, Korea, and Thailand) protested the Byrd Amendment and requested consultations with the United States under Article 14 of the WTO Dispute Settlement Understanding. When these consultations did not resolve the dispute, these same countries called in July 2001 for the formation of a WTO dispute settlement panel. Canada and Mexico later joined with this call for a panel. After considering the case, the WTO panel ruled that the Byrd Amendment violates WTO rules.[43]

The United States government has responded to this WTO ruling in two ways. At the urging of many in Congress, the United States Trade Representative appealed the ruling at the WTO. At the same time, the Bush administration urged that Congress reconsider the law and move toward repeal.[44] To date the situation remains unresolved. However, one thing seems clear. This is that if the Byrd Amendment is allowed to stand it will add a new dimension to American antidumping practice that will benefit United States producers and provide them with another incentive to file antidumping cases. One might also conclude that if the Byrd Amendment survives, other countries will quickly copy the new American practice and the result will be a proliferation of such rules among WTO members. In turn, this will no doubt have constricting effects on international commerce.

American Countervailing Duty Rules

The second set of United States unfair trade laws considered in this chapter has to do with the countervailing duties that are imposed to offset the subsidies that foreign governments sometimes use to promote exports. The nature of these governmental subsidies has changed considerably over the years since the United States first set up laws to counter such practices, but in general a subsidy may be understood as a transfer of resources from the government to a private firm that is designed to allow that firm to compete more effectively in international commerce.

The discussion herein of American CVD legislation begins with an examination of the reasons such laws were initially passed and continues by considering how these laws have shifted from their original purposes to become far more protective in recent years. As will be seen, CVD rules and procedures have followed a path that is similar to the one followed by AD laws and have been affected by many of the same forces. That is, the lowering of American tariffs in the years after the passage of the Reciprocal Trade Agreements Act of 1934 and the trade agreements created by the GATT and the WTO have had strong effects on United States CVD regulations. However, one key difference does exist between American AD and CVD laws. This has to do with the effects that antitrust considerations had on early antidumping laws, for one finds no parallel antitrust effects on CVD legislation.

Early Countervailing Duty Laws

The first American countervailing duty law was enacted in the Tariff Act of 1890 (referred to as the McKinley Tariff). This legislation imposed a countervailing duty on all refined sugar that came from any country that directly or indirectly granted a bounty to those who exported sugar. This countervailing duty was in addition to the ordinary tariff that applied to sugar. Under the provisions of this law, the duty imposed was uniform, with all refined sugar from bounty-granting countries receiving the same duty, regardless of the amount of the bounty granted. Such a provision was considered necessary because several European countries, most notably France, Germany, and Austria, were notorious for the bounties they provided for their exporters, especially those who sold agricultural goods abroad.[45] The American legislation was designed to protect United States sugar producers from the untoward effects of such practices, which were regarded as confronting Americans with an unacceptable degree of international competition.

The 1890 countervailing duty law was extended twice before the turn of the century. The first extension was in the Tariff Act of 1894 (the Wilson-Gorman Tariff), which, in addition to levying the duty on sugar, authorized the Treasury Department to suspend the duty if a foreign producer could prove that it had received no export bounty. The second was in the Tariff Act of 1897 (the Dingley Tariff), which imposed a duty to counter the bounties on any goods entering the United States. The 1897 law also gave the Secretary of the Treasury the authority to adjust the countervailing duty in order to offset the level of the bounty.[46] Thus, the 1897 legislation was the first to go beyond the uniform duty approach in an attempt to fine tune CVDs to ensure that they properly offset the benefits foreigners received from their governments.

The new American law followed Belgian legislation passed in 1892 that used similar procedures to handle subsidized imports. Over the course of the next three decades, India (in 1899), Switzerland (1902), Serbia (1904), Spain (1906), France (1910), Japan (1910), British South Africa (1914), Portugal (1921), and New Zealand (1921) passed their own countervailing duty laws. Most of these laws differed from the 1897 American law in one key respect, for while the American law left the president with no discretion when it came to the imposition of CVDs, for the most part, the foreign laws made CVDs subject to an executive decision.[47]

The Tariff Acts of 1909 (the Payne-Aldrich Tariff) and 1913 (the Underwood Tariff) retained the approach to CVDs found in the Tariff Act of 1897. The Underwood Tariff did expand the reach of American CVD legislation in one important way, however, for it applied countervailing duties to the bounties or grants paid by provincial governments and other political subdivisions found in foreign countries.[48] Thus, on the eve of World War I the United States had what were widely regarded as the toughest countervailing duty laws in the world. One feature that made American laws so tough was the lack of executive discretion when it came to imposing duties. In addition, by 1913 the United States was taking the lead in expanding the definition of bounties to include payments from local governments. And the actual application of American law extended the scope of what was treated as a bounty even further, for a federal appeals court ruled in 1901 and the United States Supreme Court ruled in 1903 and 1919 that foreign tax remissions and tax refunds on exported goods constituted bounties covered by American CVD legislation.[49]

Additional pre–World War II legislative moves pertaining to CVDs are found in the Tariff Act of 1922 (the Fordney-McCumber Tariff) and the

Tariff Act of 1930 (the Smoot-Hawley Tariff). Under the Fordney-McCumber Tariff, the definition of a bounty or grant was extended yet again to include direct or indirect payments by a government, one of its colonies, or by a political subdivision to subsidize the manufacturing and production of goods and to include as well both private and public export bounties. This new definition expanded the reach of CVDs beyond export bounties to include payments that defrayed production costs. In the 1930 law, section 303 authorized the Treasury Department to estimate when necessary the levels of export subsidies, a move that handed American investigators a substantial amount of discretion. Hence, American CVD rules continued to be seen as the most stringent in the world, for they not only had the above characteristics, but there also was no injury test associated with the application of CVDs, for the administration of foreign bounties and grants were regarded ipso facto as acts that automatically harmed United States producers.[50]

Countervailing Duties and the GATT

Section 303 of the Tariff Act of 1930 remained unaltered as the guidepost for American CVD rules until the Trade Act of 1974 was passed. One function of the 1974 law was to authorize American participation in the Tokyo Round of GATT negotiations. While writing this legislation, Congress made several changes to United States CVD procedures. The first established time limits for the Treasury Department when conducting subsidy investigations. It was stipulated that a preliminary determination should be made within six months and a final decision within one year. These limits were enacted in response to complaints from American special interests that the Treasury Department was slow in responding to the cases they filed. A second change extended American CVD rules to cover non-dutiable imports. Previously only dutiable imports were covered. Finally, section 516 of the Tariff Act of 1930 was amended to provide American producers who were dissatisfied with the outcome of a Treasury Department CVD investigation with the right to file a petition calling for a review. This change gave American producers the same right to appeal adverse decisions that foreign producers had possessed for some time.[51]

The next set of changes in American CVD rules came in the Trade Agreements Act of 1979. As was mentioned earlier in this chapter, this law was designed to enact the trade agreements the United States reached during the Tokyo Round of GATT negotiations. As far as CVDs were concerned, four major alterations were made in 1979. The first was found in section 101 of the 1979 law. This section set up a title VII in the Tariff Act of 1930 to extend an injury test in CVD investigations to all imports, dutiable and non-dutiable, from parties to the GATT. The new Tokyo Round Subsidies Code (which was voluntary) suggested such a change. The injury test did not apply to imports from parties that did not subscribe to the GATT.[52]

A second change shifted the authority for conducting CVD investigations from the Treasury Department to the Commerce Department. As was the case with dumping investigations, where a similar change in authority was made, this alteration reflected the Congressional belief that the Commerce Department would be more diligent in conducting investigations.[53]

The third set of changes also was meant to tighten CVD investigations by providing both for more stringent time limits for preliminary CVD determinations and for annual reviews of CVD rates to guarantee that they would be maintained at the appropriate levels.[54] These time limits and reviews quickly became a source of irritation for countries under investigation because it left them with severely restricted amounts of time for filling out CVD questionnaires and meant that they were subject to continuing reexaminations of their subsidy practices.

The final change in CVD procedures in 1979 involved the use of best information available (BIA). As was noted above when discussing dumping, one of the foremost problems confronting American investigations in unfair trade cases was (and is) the acquisition of appropriate information. The 1979 law attempted to solve this problem and short-circuit attempts to stall American CVD investigations by allowing the Commerce Department to use such information as it could get when conducting its analysis. This authorization to use BIA generally was regarded abroad as greatly increasing the probability of a positive CVD finding and became a source of grave concern for those confronting American investigations.[55]

One change recommended by the Tokyo Round Subsidies Code that Congress refused to make had to do with the definition of what constituted a subsidy. While the Tokyo Round Code recommended that the subsidized loans and loan guarantees governments gave to private firms should not be seen as a subsidy, Congress specified that such arrangements would be subject to CVDs without exception.[56]

By the early 1980s, the recession confronting the United States economy and the challenge posed by Japanese and other foreign competition led American special interests to call for changes in United States CVD laws. One issue that arose during this debate related to possible revisions in the definition of what constituted a subsidy. Noting that many foreign governments maintained special programs under which those who produced basic raw materials and other primary products received governmental assistance, several American groups called for redefining the term subsidy to include such programs, particularly when the primary products were used as inputs for finished goods that were exported to the United States.[57] One example of a primary product subsidy is found in the agricultural assistance programs many countries have to assist their farmers. Other American producers called for treating as subsidies the industrial policies practiced by such countries as Japan. The logic behind labeling an industrial policy as a subsidy was found in the notion that the governmental advice and other assistance provided constituted a form of aid that gave the recipient an unfair advantage over American producers.[58]

While proposals of these types were widely discussed and caused considerable controversy, the Reagan administration refused to include them in any trade-related legislation. Congress was able to include a provision in the Trade and Tariff Act of 1984, however, that called for the Department of Commerce, the Department of Labor, the United States Trade Representative (USTR), and the Comptroller General of the United States to prepare by June 1, 1985, studies examining the issue of industrial policy and its relationship to the question of subsidies.[59]

In addition, section 613 of the 1984 law included a provision to guard against upstream subsidies. An upstream subsidy was defined as a payment from a government or a customs union that covered an input product used in making merchandise that is subject to a countervailing duty, that confers a competitive benefit on that merchandise, and that has a significant effect on the cost of producing the merchandise.[60] An example of an upstream subsidy would be bicycles produced with subsidized steel. While the production or sale of the final product, the bicycles, might not receive any form of government assistance, the fact that they are produced with subsidized steel was regarded by many in Congress as conferring an unfair advantage that required a countervailing duty correction.

The upstream subsidy provision extended American CVD rules into new territory that was not covered by the Tokyo Round Subsidies Code. As such, it became the source of considerable trouble between the United States and its GATT trading partners, many of whom felt the that the legislation left the terms "competitive benefit" and "significant effect" undefined and gave the Commerce Department a considerable range of discretion when it came to applying the new rules.[61]

Another major provision in the 1984 law that pertained to CVDs had to do with cumulation. As was the case with regard to dumping (see above), a new standard was set for determining injury during CVD investigations. Whereas the previous standard allowed the ITC considerable leeway in deciding when to cumulate during injury investigations, the new cumulation rule set a tougher standard that required cumulation in almost all cases. As was described earlier, this greatly enhanced both the likelihood that American producers would file complaints and the probability of a positive injury determination.[62]

The lobbying to extend the reach of American countervailing duty laws continued during the second Reagan administration as Congress prepared to pass the Omnibus Trade and Competitiveness Act (OTCA) in 1988. As a result, that law included several new provisions relating to CVDs. The first once again expanded the definition of what constituted a subsidy. Under previous definitions, subsidies were regarded as governmental transfers of resources that allowed foreign producers to produce and export their goods more easily. In section 1312 of the 1988 law, this definition was altered to include what were referred to as "domestic subsidies." A domestic subsidy was defined as including any benefit provided by a foreign government to its producers, even if obtaining the benefit did not depend upon the recipient's export performance. An example of a domestic subsidy would be the reduced utility rates governments often charge to certain industries.[63]

Many American producers argued that domestic subsidies allowed their foreign competitors to operate with far lower overheads and that this in turn meant that these foreign corporations could sell goods in the United States at extremely low prices. Most members of Congress agreed with this view and regarded amending American CVD laws to include domestic subsidies as merely creating a "level playing field" in international commerce. Foreign governments and corporations, however, protested the new American law as an unreasonable extension of the reach of United States CVD rules.

A second feature of the OTCA relating to CVDs permitted the USTR to exclude countries from the injury part of a CVD investigation if it was determined that the country was failing to live up to its obligations under the Tokyo Round Subsidies Code. This move, which is found in section 1314, was a reaction to a proposal from the Trade Reform Action Committee, a group of American businesses concerned with imports and competition. This Action Committee was especially interested in the textile imports coming from Brazil and India, both of which countries were accused of ignoring both the Tokyo Round Code and the obligations incurred under the Multi-Fiber Arrangement (MFA) to regulate international commerce in textiles.[64]

The third change in American CVD rules that came in 1988 resulted from a controversy over imports of pork from Canada. This dispute began in 1985 when the Commerce Department refused to apply the upstream subsidies provision in the Trade and Tariff Act of 1984 to the sale of Canadian pork in the United States. After the United States Court of International Trade overruled this Commerce Department decision in April 1987, Congress sought to clarify the issue by stating in section 1313 of the OTCA that the subsidies provided for raw agricultural goods should be considered when examining finished agricultural products.[65]

The final major CVD-related provision in the OTCA had to do with cumulation. As was mentioned above, in 1984 Congress created the cumulation rule for injury tests in AD and CVD cases. By 1988, the Commerce Department complained that as written the cumulation rule was confronting its International Trade Administration (ITA) with an undue burden in CVD investigations since the rule required the full-scale examination of even minimal levels of imports. In response, section 1330(b) of the OTCA stated that negligible imports from any particular country need not be included in CVD investigations if the International Trade Commission determined that they did not contribute to the harm done to American producers. The law left the definition of negligible unclear, but directed the ITC to apply the rule narrowly.[66]

The Uruguay Round Subsidies Agreement

During the Uruguay Round of GATT negotiations, the question of subsidies received prominent treatment. As can be seen from the discussion above, many aspects of American CVD laws were regarded by other countries as questionable. Controversy also surrounded the CVD laws found in Australia, Canada, the European Union, Japan, and elsewhere. At the same time, many producers in the United States and in other parts of the world felt that they faced unacceptably stiff international competition because of the subsidies many foreign governments provided to their domestic industries. The result was intense negotiations regarding such issues as what types of government support programs would be allowed under WTO/GATT rules and whether poorer societies should be accorded special privileges.

When the final WTO Agreement on Subsidies and Countervailing Measures was completed in 1994, it had at its heart what is known as the "traffic light" approach. To understand the traffic light approach, one must first consider how the WTO defines a subsidy. Articles 1 and 2 of the Subsidies Agreement state that a subsidy is a financial contribution or any form of income or price support provided by "a government or any public body" that "involves a direct transfer of funds," results in the government forgoing revenue that is otherwise due, leads to the provision to local producers of "goods or services other than general infrastructure," results in governmental purchases of goods without allowing for open bidding, and confers a benefit. In order to be actionable (that is, subject to CVDs) under WTO rules, this transfer of resources or benefits must be given to a specific economic entity by a country's central government. This is known as the rule of "specificity."[67] As can be seen from the previous discussion of how the United States has defined subsidies over the years, this WTO definition conformed closely to American views regarding what is and is not a subsidy.

The WTO traffic light approach to subsidies was designed to distinguish between actionable and non-actionable subsidies (in American terminology the terms used are countervailable and non-countervailable). According to the traffic light system, a "red light" subsidy, which is prohibited under all circumstances, is one that is contingent on export performance (known as an export subsidy) or that requires a domestic producer to use domestic goods instead of imported goods when assembling a product (referred to as an import substitution subsidy). Red light subsidies are always actionable under WTO rules. When a country decides to file a complaint over a red light subsidy within the WTO dispute settlement system it simply needs to prove that such a subsidy exists, but is not required to demonstrate injury to a domestic producer. However, WTO rules do require an injury test before a country can impose a CVD to counter a red light subsidy.[68]

The second traffic light category is dark amber. Dark amber subsidies mirror what American CVD rules refer to as domestic subsidies. While these subsidies are not prohibited, they are actionable if they adversely affect another WTO member by harming a domestic industry, by seriously prejudicing a member's ability to sell in a third country market, or by nullifying or impairing the benefits due under the 1994 GATT agreement.[69] WTO guidelines in Article 6.1 of the Subsidies Agreement for evaluating whether a subsidy is dark amber include: (1) a subsidy that exceeds 5 percent ad valorem, (2) subsidies that are designed to cover an industry's or an enterprise's operating losses, and (3) the direct forgiveness of a debt.[70] Under WTO rules, members may offer compensation to other members when they are judged to have actionable dark amber subsidy programs. Such compensation would be offered as an alternative to the imposition of CVDs by the affected party. It should be noted that affected parties are not required to accept the compensation.[71]

Green light subsidies were defined in Article 8 of the Subsidies Agreement as non-actionable. These subsidies fall into three categories: (1) subsidies for industrial research and development (civil aircraft are excluded from this category), (2) subsidies to disadvantaged regions, and (3) subsidies designed to meet new environmental regulations. Article 31 of the Subsidies Agreement states that the green light category only would remain in effect for five years after the WTO was established in 1994.[72]

The final traffic light category is for yellow light subsidies. This is a resid-ual label that applies to all subsidies that are not included in any of the above categories. As a result, the question as to whether these subsidies are action-able is open. It is, however, up to the complainant to offer sufficient evidence to demonstrate that a yellow light subsidy should be subject to duties.

A second major feature of the Uruguay Round Subsidies Agreement re-lates to special and differential treatment for developing countries.[73] Most of these special provisions are found in Article 27. These rules begin by stating in Article 27.2 that the WTO prohibition on export subsidies does not ap-ply to the developing country members of the WTO unless the production in question attains "export competitiveness" status. This means that the product must be capable of taking sales away from like goods produced in ad-vanced countries and that the product acquires a specified share of global trade. This exemption is good for eight years, with Article 27.4 providing for the possibility of renewal if a country makes such a request. If a product is ex-port competitive, then its subsidy must be phased out over a two-year period. For the least developed countries, the exemption from the prohibition on ex-port subsidies has no time limit unless the good in question attains export competitiveness. For export competitive goods, there is an eight-year phase out period.[74]

Developing countries also are exempt under Article 27.3 from the ban on import substitution subsidies. Once again, this exemption is temporary, last-ing for eight years for the least developed countries and five years for other developing countries. Again, renewals are available upon application. Fi-nally, Article 27.13 states that the debt forgiveness of developing country governments will not be treated as an actionable subsidy if it is linked to a privatization program.

A second feature of special and differential treatment pertains to how the WTO system handles disputes relating to developing country subsidies. Whereas the dispute system automatically regards red light subsidies of ad-vanced country members as actionable, the same is not the case for develop-ing countries. Instead, Articles 27.7 and 27.8 of the Subsidies Agreement state that during the eight year transition period (which, as noted above, can be extended) the red light subsidies granted by developing countries only are actionable in the WTO dispute settlement system if the complainant can of-fer positive proof that the subsidy in question has resulted in serious damage to a domestic industry. Further, Article 27.9 says that developing country subsidies that result in the displacement of advanced country exports to third markets are not actionable. For example, if subsidized pottery exports from Peru displace American pottery exports to Spain, no action can be taken.

A third special treatment offered to developing countries relates to de minimis levels. To recall, a deminimis level is the amount of a subsidy that terminates a countervailing duty investigation. For advanced countries, the de minimis level is set by the Subsidies Agreement at 1 percent or less. For the least developed countries, the de minimis subsidy is 3 percent or less for the eight-year transition period (which can be renewed). For other developing countries, de minimis is 2 percent or less, with the possibility of an increase to 3 percent if a country eliminates its export subsidies before the end of the eight-year transition period.[75]

The final major special provision for developing countries pertains to cumulation. As was explained earlier in this chapter, cumulation rules allow for damage assessments due to subsidies to be based on the effects of the total subsidized imports of a good instead of simply on the effects of the subsidized goods in any specific case under investigation. Under the Subsidies Agreement, developing countries are exempt from cumulation rules as long as their exports account for less than 4 percent of the total imports of the good in question into the affected country. Additionally, it is specified in the Agreement that the collective total imports from countries that are individually covered by the 4 percent rule may not exceed 9 percent of the total imports of the good. For advanced countries, the respective cumulation amounts are 3 percent and 7 percent, as in the Antidumping Agreement.

An additional issue relating to the WTO has to do with its dispute settlement system. During the Uruguay Round, a new Dispute Settlement Understanding was set up that allows any WTO member to challenge the trade-related behavior of another member if that other member is thought to be in violation of WTO rules. A WTO panel may then be created to evaluate the arguments presented by each side and to issue a ruling regarding the proper interpretation of WTO rules. The dispute settlement system also can issue judgments regarding the penalties to be assessed against violators. This system relates to the subsidy problem (and to dumping) in that it gives members an avenue for challenging the CVD (and AD) decisions made by other members. Smaller and less developed countries benefit especially from the system because they have an international arena for airing such problems as they may confront.[76]

The Uruguay Round Agreements Act and the Byrd Amendment

Having outlined the WTO Subsidies Agreement, attention can now turn to a brief description of how the Uruguay Round Agreements Act (URAA) of 1994 incorporated the Subsidies Agreement into American law. Title II of the URAA amended the provisions in the Tariff Act of 1930 as they relate to countervailing measures. Section 251 of the URAA and section 771(5) of the 1930 law set the definitions of "subsidy" and "countervailable subsidy" as they are found in Article 1 of the Subsidies Agreement. In section 771(5A) of the 1930 law one finds the counterpart in American law to the WTO prohibition of red light subsidies, while section 771(5B) deals with green light subsidies. Section 281(c) of the URAA lays out the procedures for handling dark amber subsidies.[77]

As far as special and differential treatment for developing countries is concerned, the URAA focuses its attention on questions relating to de minimis levels and cumulation. The URAA amends section 703 of the Tariff Act of 1930 to establish American subsidy de minimis levels at the amounts specified in the Subsidies Agreement. Section 771(24)(B) of the 1930 law deals with putting American cumulation rules in line with the requirements of the Subsidies Agreement. Another provision relating to developing countries is found in section 267 of the URAA. This section deals with the issue of allowing developing countries to obtain special treatment with regard to red light subsidies.[78]

Additional issues in the URAA that relate to subsidies include the provision adding section 751(c)(1) to the Tariff Act of 1930 to require sunset reviews. These reviews are conducted according to the same rules that are employed in AD sunset reviews (see above). Beyond this, Title 1 subtitle c of the URAA specifies the procedures under which the United States participates in the WTO dispute settlement system. These procedures are the same as those described earlier when discussing antidumping.[79]

One final matter regarding recent American CVD legislation has to do with the Byrd Amendment, which was described above in the section on antidumping. Under the terms of this law, the duties collected to offset foreign subsidy programs are distributed to the affected American producers.[80] As was mentioned previously, this provision is extremely controversial abroad and has been challenged in the WTO dispute settlement system, where it was ruled a violation of WTO rules. At present the executive and legislative branches of the U.S. government are debating the best means for resolving the situation.

Antidumping and Countervailing Duty Investigation Timetables

Before turning to the chapter summary, a brief description of the stages involved in AD and CVD investigations is in order. In addition, it is important to mention the timetables associated with each stage. Issues relating to the procedures and deadlines relating to AD and CVD investigations have been very controversial over the years. There are two sources for this controversy, one domestic, the other foreign. Domestic complaints usually argue that American producers suffer unacceptable damage from dumped or subsidized foreign goods while they wait for the Commerce Department and the United States International Trade Commission (ITC) to conduct their inquiries. As far as foreigners are concerned, it often is alleged that American investigations are timed in such a way as to inflict unreasonable harm on foreigners by keeping them under the cloud of investigation for as long as possible. In addition, foreigners maintain that investigation timetables give them little time to respond properly to American requests for information, which can result in the use of the best information available, a procedure that almost always works to the disadvantage of foreigners.

For the most part, Congress has responded to the above complaints by seeking to alter American regulations to suit the interests of domestic businesses. This is as might be expected, given the highly political nature of the issue. As was noted above, one of the first Congressional moves to amend unfair trade investigation timetables came in the Trade Act of 1974, which set a six month limit on the initial Treasury Department investigations and a twelve month overall limit. A second change came in the Trade Agreements Act of 1979 when the limit on preliminary investigations was reduced to eighty-five days.

The Trade and Tariff Act of 1984 divided the preliminary investigation into two parts, granting the Commerce Department's International Trade Administration (ITA) 20 days to determine whether a case has merit and the ITC 45 days to decide whether there is reason to believe that an American producer has been harmed. If either of these questions is answered negatively, the case ends. If both answers are positive, then the 1984 law allowed the ITA and the ITC between 40 and 105 days in CVD cases and between 115 and 165 days in AD cases to finish their preliminary investigations. When the time allowed for final determinations is added to the amounts allowed for the preliminary phase, the 1984 law permitted AD investigations to consume anywhere from 280 to 420 days. For CVD investigations, the corresponding amounts of time ranged between 205 and 300 days.[81]

In the Uruguay Round Agreements Act (URAA) of 1994, the above time limits were altered somewhat. The URAA retained the two-stage investigation found in earlier legislation. It also continues to stipulate that the ITA and the ITC will conduct unfair trade investigations, with the ITA handling the analysis of whether dumping or subsidies have occurred, and the ITC the question of injury. The early phases of the investigation remain as specified by the 1984 law, for the ITA has 20 days to determine whether cases have merit, and the ITC has 45 days to decide whether injury is likely. The primary difference between the 1984 and 1994 timetables is found in adjustments that reduce the remaining parts of the investigation timetables. Under the new rules, AD cases may take between 280 and 390 days to complete, and CVD cases may last for between 205 and 270 days. These time limits are slightly shorter than under the 1984 law.[82]

One key point when considering these timetables is that the respondent in an AD or CVD case usually receives the questionnaire that requests information about its business practices 30 days after the case is initiated. This questionnaire is over one hundred pages in length and requires complex and detailed responses. Once the respondent has the questionnaire, 30 days are allowed for an answer, with there being the possibility of a 15-day extension. Thus, AD and CVD investigations place considerable pressure on respondents because they have limited amounts of time to develop their cases. At the same time, the fact that unfair cases can last up to 390 days leaves respondents under the pressure of investigation for lengthy periods of time.[83] As one can imagine, foreigners have a strong dislike for the way this timetable is set up and regard it as yet another way in which American unfair trade regulations work to their disadvantage.

Chapter Summary

This chapter examined American antidumping and countervailing duty laws. The origins and evolutionary paths of both sets of laws were described, as was their relationship with the rules established at the conclusion of the Uruguay Round of GATT negotiations when the WTO was established. As has been discussed, American AD and CVD rules were established at the end of the nineteenth century and during the early part of the twentieth century. The AD laws were first set up to handle the problem of possible antitrust violations on the part of foreigners selling goods in the United States market. Early CVD legislation was aimed at the export bounties some European countries employed to promote their products in foreign markets.

In the years before World War II, both sets of laws changed significantly. The changes in AD rules focused on a shift from a prosecutorial enforcement approach to an administrative approach that was based on the imposition of special tariffs (referred to as antidumping duties) that were designed to negate the benefits of dumping. With regard to subsidies, the change involved a shift from a single catchall duty on imports from bounty granting countries to a process that allowed the Treasury Department to estimate the price benefit foreign goods received due to a subsidy and to offset that benefit by imposing a duty (known as a countervailing duty).

In the years after World War II, American AD and CVD laws underwent even more changes. Two factors account for most of these alterations. The first was the continual lowering of United States tariffs in response to negotiations under the Reciprocal Trade Agreements program and during GATT rounds of talks. The second was the rules developed during the Kennedy, Tokyo, and Uruguay Rounds of GATT negotiations that were designed to regulate national AD and CVD rules and procedures.

Lower American tariffs primarily affected United States AD and CVD laws by encouraging American producers who feared foreign competition to push for more inclusive unfair trade regulations. The motive behind such demands was the desire to obtain the greatest degree of protection possible from one of the only avenues left open after negotiations lowered tariffs. This avenue was the route that took those seeking protection down the unfair trade road. This approach remained a viable protectionist device because the United States treated dumping and subsidies as unfair trade that still could be restricted even as other limits on trade were disappearing as the GATT reduced American tariffs.

The reach of American AD and CVD laws was extended continually from the 1950s to the present. This was done for the most part by expanding the legal definitions of dumping and subsidies. Thus, dumping was continually redefined to move it away from its predatory pricing origins to include first sales in which the American price differed from foreign prices and eventually any act of selling below cost. For subsidies, the original focus on export bounties was expanded to include such things as domestic subsidies and upstream subsidies.

Another device that increased the effects of American unfair trade laws had to do with the data gathering techniques that were permitted. Since pricing and subsidies information often were difficult to acquire, Congress progressively allowed American investigators first to construct (that is, estimate) prices and later to use the best information available during investigations. Cumulation rules also were created. These changes greatly increased the probability that foreign behavior would be treated as problematic.

A third technique that expanded the impact of United States AD and CVD rules was a shift of authority for conducting investigations from the Treasury Department to the Commerce Department. This happened in 1979. Such a move was prompted by the lax attention to unfair trade that Congress believed characterized the Treasury Department and by the perception that

reshuffling bureaucratic responsibilities would lead to a more vigorous enforcement of the law. The fact that the president never has been given the
authority to set aside or alter unfair trade decisions also plays an important
part in enforcement. The absence of presidential authority means that competing national interests and pressures from foreign governments have little
effect on the decision to impose either antidumping or countervailing duties.

The international trade agreements reached during the Kennedy, Tokyo,
and Uruguay Rounds of GATT negotiations have tended to work against the
expansion of the use of AD and CVD processes. In the Kennedy and Tokyo
Rounds, GATT codes were developed that called for injury tests before duties could be assessed. Both codes were voluntary. Congress rejected the
Kennedy Round suggestion, but accepted the Tokyo Round code under restricted conditions.

The Uruguay Round Antidumping and Subsidies Agreements placed additional restrictions on the handling of unfair trade. For one thing, the new
rules are no longer voluntary. For another, sunset reviews are required. In addition, de minimis and cumulation rules were set up to limit the occasions
upon which duties could be applied and a dispute settlement system was created to deal with conflicts pertaining to AD and CVD enforcement. Developing countries also were designated for special treatment. However, the sum
of the new WTO unfair trade regulations has had little more than a marginal
effect on how the United States handles its AD and CVD cases.

A final point regarding AD and CVD regulations has to do with their use
to harass international competitors. Many foreign governments and foreign
corporations have complained for years that United States unfair trade laws
are designed to encourage American firms to file cases that can be used to restrict the ability of foreigners to do business in the United States. The continual expansion of the reach of these laws, as described above, give this
claim some credibility. The lengthy and complex investigation process also
reinforces this claim. On top of this, one must consider the provisions of the
controversial Byrd Amendment, an act that offers substantial monetary benefits to those who file AD and CVD cases. Thus, it seems reasonably safe to
conclude that American AD and CVD laws can be and are used to torment
one's international competitors.

Having described American AD and CVD rules and procedures, attention
can now shift to an examination of the difficulties developing countries face
when they confront accusations relating to unfair trade in the United States.
The next chapter examines this question by looking at the manner in which
the Thai government and Thai businesses handle the problems associated
with American AD and CVD investigations.

Notes

1. John M. Rothgeb, Jr., *U.S. Trade Policy: Balancing Economic Dreams and Political Realities*, Washington, DC: CQ Press, 2001, p. 95.

2. Congressional Budget Office (CBO), *How the GATT Affects U.S. Antidumping and Countervailing-Duty Policy*, Washington, DC: Congressional Budget Office, 1994, p. 16.

3. Jacob Viner, *Dumping: A Problem in International Trade*, Chicago: University of Chicago Press, 1925 (reprint New York: Sentry Press, 1966), pp. 239–40.

4. CBO, *How the GATT Affects*, pp. 16–17.

5. Ibid., p. 18.

6. Viner, *Dumping: A Problem in International Trade*, p. 240. It should be noted that the courts ruled that the Sherman Act did apply if import contracts were signed in the United States. If the contracts were signed abroad, then the law did not apply.

7. Ibid., pp. 240–41; CBO, *How the GATT Affects*, pp. 19–20. The quote is from the CBO, *How the GATT Affects*, p. 19.

8. Michael J. Finger, "The Origins and Evolution of Antidumping Regulations," in *Antidumping: How It Works and Who Gets Hurt*, ed. Michael J. Finger, Ann Arbor: University of Michigan Press, 1993, p. 19; William H. Lash, *U.S. International Trade Regulation: A Primer*, Washington, DC: The AEI Press, 1998, p. 25; Alfred A. Eckes, "U.S. Trade History," in *U.S. Trade Policy: History, Theory, and the WTO*, ed. William A. Lovelt, Alfred E. Eckes, and Richard L. Brinkman, Armonk, NY: M.E. Sharpe, 1999, p. 67. The quote is from CBO, *How the GATT Affects*, p. 20.

9. U.S. House of Representatives, Committee on Ways and Means, *Overview and Compilation of U.S. Trade Statutes*, Washington, DC: U.S. Government Printing Office, 2001, p. 618.

10. CBO, *How the GATT Affects*, p. 20; Lash, *U.S. International Trade Regulation*, p. 25; Eckes, "U.S. Trade History," p. 67.

11. Lash, *U.S. International Trade Regulation*, p. 25; Greg Mastel, *Antidumping Laws and the U.S. Economy*, Armonk, NY: M.E. Sharpe, 1998, p. 19. It should be noted that the Tariff Commission was renamed the International Trade Commission in 1974.

12. Mastel, *Antidumping Laws and the U.S. Economy*, p. 19; CBO, *How the GATT Affects*, p. 21; Eckes, "U.S. Trade History," pp. 67–68.

13. U.S. House of Representatives, *Overview and Compilation*, pp. 91–92; CBO, *How the GATT Affects*, p. 21.

14. U.S. House of Representatives, *Amendments to the Antidumping Act of 1921, As Amended*, July 1957, pp. 12–14.

15. Mastel, *Antidumping and the U.S. Economy*, pp. 19–21.

16. Stephen L. Lande and Craig VanGrasstek, *The Trade and Tariff Act of 1984: Trade Policy in the Reagan Administration*, Lexington, MA: D.C. Heath and Co., 1986, p. 108; Mastel, *Antidumping Laws and the U.S. Economy*, p. 21; U.S. Congress, *Tariff Act of 1930*, 71st Congress, 2nd session, Public Law no. 361, Washington, DC: U.S. Government Printing Office, p. 127.

17. The Reciprocal Trade Agreements program was first approved by Congress in 1934 and regularly renewed thereafter until 1962. Under this program, the president was authorized to negotiate agreements with other countries to lower tariffs on a product-by-product basis. The law required that all such agreements be set up according to strict reciprocity so that any tariff reductions granted by the United States would be matched by the reductions of other countries. The deals reached under the program were extended to other American trading partners on a most favored nation basis and led to a slow, but continual, decrease in U.S. protectionism.

18. Greyson Bryan, *Taxing Unfair International Trade Practice: A Study of U.S. Antidumping and Countervailing Duty Laws*, Lexington, MA: Lexington Books, 1980, pp. 8–9; U.S. House of Representatives, *Amendments to the Antidumping Act of 1921, As Amended*, July 1957, p. 14; U.S. House of Representatives, *Overview and Compilation*, p. 90.

19. Bryan, *Taxing Unfair International Trade*, p. 9.

20. CBO, *How the GATT Affects*, p. 26.

21. Pietro S. Nivola, *Regulating Unfair Trade*, Washington, DC: Brookings Institution, 1993, pp. 92–93; CBO, *How the GATT Affects*, p. 25.

22. CBO, *How the GATT Affects*, pp. 24, 26, 27; U.S. House of Representatives, *Overview and Compilation*, pp. 90–91.

23. U.S. House of Representatives, *Overview and Compilation*, p. 91; CBO, *How the GATT Affects*, p. 27.

24. Ibid.

25. Nivola, *Regulating Unfair Trade*, pp. 94–95; CBO, *How the GATT Affects*, p. 28.

26. Nivola, *Regulating Unfair Trade*, p. 97.

27. Ibid., p. 99; U.S. Congress, *Omnibus Trade and Tariff Act of 1984*, Public Law 98-573, Bill Summary and Status for 98th Congress (available from http://thomas.loc.gov), p. 10; Lande and Van Grasstek, *The Trade and Tariff Act of 1984*, pp. 121–22; John H. Jackson, *The World Trading System: Law and Policy of International Economic Relations*, Cambridge, MA: MIT Press, 1997, pp. 270–71.

28. Lande and Van Grasstek, *The Trade and Tariff Act of 1984*, p. 119; the quote is from U.S. Congress, *Omnibus Trade and Tariff Act of 1984*, Bill Summary and Status, p. 10.

29. Lande and Van Grasstek, *The Trade and Tariff Act of 1984*, pp. 119–20; CBO, *How the GATT Affects*, p. 28.

30. Lande and Van Grasstek, *The Trade and Tariff Act of 1984*, p. 124; U.S. Congress, *Omnibus Trade and Tariff Act of 1984*, Bill Summary and Status, p. 11; CBO, *How the GATT Affects*, p. 28.

31. Nivola, *Regulating Unfair Trade*, p. 105; U.S. House of Representatives, *Overview and Compilation*, pp. 102–3; U.S. Congress, *Omnibus Trade and Competitiveness Act of 1988*, Public Law 100-418, Bill Summary and Status for 100th Congress (available from http://thomas.loc.gov), pp. 5–6.

32. For a discussion of the problems confronting the semiconductor industry, see Rothgeb, *U.S. Trade Policy*, pp. 187–90.

33. U.S. House of Representatives, *Overview and Compilation*, p. 93, 616–17; U.S. Congress, *Omnibus Trade and Competitiveness Act of 1988*, Bill Summary and Status, p. 5; CBO, *How the GATT Affects*, p. 29; Gary N. Horlick and Geoffrey D. Oliver, "Antidumping and Countervailing Duty Provisions of the Omnibus Trade and Competitiveness Act of 1988," *Journal of World Trade*, vol. 23, June 1989, p. 18.

34. Developing country concerns over antidumping rules were not confined to the United States. Many of these countries also complained about the European Union, Canada, and other advanced countries.

35. U.S. Department of Commerce, International Trade Administration, *Statement of Administrative Action, Agreement on Implementation of Article VI* (available from http://ia.ita.doc.gov), p. 13; U.S. House of Representatives, *Overview and Compilation*, p. 91.

36. U.S. Congress, *Public Law 103-465, Uruguay Round Agreements Act*, December 8, 1994, section 213 (a)(3); U.S. Department of Commerce, International Trade Administration, *Statement of Administrative Action, Agreement on Implementation of Article VI*, p. 34. It should be noted that due to a lack of clarity in the Uruguay Round Antidumping Agreement, the United States continued to employ a less than 0.5 percent de minimis during its annual reviews of AD decisions.

37. David Palmeter, "United States Implementation of the Uruguay Round Antidumping Code," *Journal of World Trade*, vol. 29, June 1995, p. 78; David Palmeter, "A Commentary on the WTO Antidumping Code," *Journal of World Trade*, vol. 30, August 1996, p. 61; U.S. Department of Commerce, International Trade Administration, *Statement of Administrative Action, Agreement on Implementation of Article VI*, p. 35; U.S. Congress, *Public Law 103-465*, section 783; U.S. House of Representatives, *Overview and Compilation*, pp. 93–94.

38. World Trade Organization, *Agreement on Implementation of Article VI of the General Agreement on Tariffs and Trade 1994*, p. 152; U.S. Congress, *Public Law 103-465*, section 222(e); U.S. Department of Commerce, International Trade Administration, *Statement of Administrative Action, Agreement on Implementation of Article VI*, p. 37.

39. David Palmeter, "United States Implementation of the Uruguay Round Antidumping Code," p. 73; Code of Federal Regulations, Title 19, "Customs Duties," Office of the Federal Register, National Archives and Records Administration, April 1, 2000, p. 218.

40. U.S. Congress, *Public Law 103-465*, section 129; U.S. House of Representatives, *Overview and Compilation*, p. 106.

41. U.S. House of Representatives, *Overview and Compilation*, p. 104; U.S. Congress, *Public Law 106-387*, October 28, 2000, title X.

42. "Bush Seeks End to Duty Payments," *Wall Street Journal*, February 4, 2003, p. A8.

43. "WTO Says U.S. Tariff Law Violates Rules," *New York Times*, July 18, 2002, p. C2; Neil King, Jr., "WTO Panel Rules Against Law on U.S. Punitive Import Duties," *Wall Street Journal*, July 18, 2002, p. A2.

44. "Bush Seeks End to Duty Payments," p. A8; "WTO Says U.S. Tariff Law Violates Rules," p. C2.

45. Viner, *Dumping: A Problem in International Trade*, pp. 168–69.

46. Ibid., p. 169.

47. CBO, *How the GATT Affects*, p. 22.

48. Bryan, *Taxing Unfair International Trade*, p. 251.

49. Viner, *Dumping: A Problem in International Trade*, pp. 173–74.

50. U.S. House of Representatives, *Tariff Act of 1922*, H.R. 7456, September 20, 1922, Washington, DC: U.S. Government Printing Office, 1922, p. 87; U.S. House of Representatives, *Overview and Compilation*, p. 84; BO, *How the GATT Affects*, p. 22; Bryan, *Taxing Unfair International Trade Practices*, p. 251.

51. Bryan, *Taxing Unfair International Trade Practices*, pp. 251–52; U.S. Congress, "The Trade Act of 1974, Public Law 93-618, 88 STAT. 1978," in *United States Code: Congressional and Administrative News*, pp. 2374–75, 2377–78; CBO, *How the GATT Affects*, p. 26.

52. U.S. Congress, "Trade Agreements Act of 1979, Public Law 96-39 [H.R. 4537]," July 26, 1979, pp. 150–51; U.S. House of Representatives, *Overview and Compilation*, p. 85.

53. U.S. House of Representatives, *Overview and Compilation*, p. 84.

54. U.S. Congress, "Trade Agreements Act of 1979," pp. 152–53; CBO, *How the GATT Affects*, p. 27.

55. U.S. Congress, "Trade Agreements Act of 1979," pp. 152–53; Nivola, *Regulating Unfair Trade*, pp. 94–95.

56. Lande and Van Grasstek, *The Trade and Tariff Act of 1984*, p. 109.

57. Ibid., p. 110.

58. Ibid., pp. 126–27.

59. Ibid., p. 127; U.S. Congress, "Trade and Tariff Act of 1984, Public Law 96-573 [H.R. 3398]," October 30, 1984, 98 STAT, p. 3042.

60. U.S. Congress, "Trade and Tariff Act of 1984," p. 3035.

61. Lande and Van Grasstek, *The Trade and Tariff Act of 1984*, pp. 126–27.

62. U.S. Congress, "Trade and Tariff Act of 1984," p. 3033.

63. Horlick and Oliver, "Antidumping and Countervailing Duty Provisions of the Omnibus Trade and Competitiveness Act of 1988," pp. 7–9; U.S. Congress, "Omnibus Trade and Competitiveness Act of 1988, Public Law 100-418 [H.R. 4848]," August 23, 1988, 102 STAT, p. 1184.

64. U.S. Congress, "Omnibus Trade and Competitiveness Act," p. 1185; Horlick and Oliver, "Antidumping and Countervailing Duty Law Provisions in the Omnibus Trade and Competitiveness Act of 1988," p. 12. It should be noted that the Multi-Fiber Arrangement was set up under GATT auspices in 1974. The MFA set quotas for almost all countries that exported textiles. The MFA operated on a product-by-product basis, setting different quotas for differing fabrics. These quotas were allowed to increase slightly each year to account for market growth.

65. U.S. Congress, "Omnibus Trade and Competitiveness Act of 1988," p. 1185; Horlick and Oliver, "Antidumping and Countervailing Duty Provisions of the Omnibus Trade and Competitiveness Act of 1988," pp. 10–11.

66. Horlick and Oliver, "Antidumping and Countervailing Duty Provisions of the Omnibus Trade and Competitiveness Act of 1988," pp. 35–37; U.S. Congress, "Omnibus Trade and Competitiveness Act of 1988," pp. 1206–1207.

67. World Trade Organization (WTO), *Agreement on Subsidies and Countervailing Measures*, pp. 229–30.

68. Ibid., pp. 231, 262; U.S. House of Representatives, *Overview and Compilation*, pp. 86–87; U.S. Department of Commerce, *Statement of Administrative Action*, *Agreement on Subsidies and Countervailing Measures*, pp. 4–5.

69. WTO, *Agreement on Subsidies and Countervailing Measures*, pp. 233–34. Serious prejudice means that the subsidies offered by another country impairs one's ability to export goods to another society where one previously had done business. An example would be a situation in which an EU subsidy on computers resulted in Egypt shifting its purchases of computers from an American firm to a European company.

70. Ibid., p. 233.

71. Raj Bhala and Kevin Kennedy, *World Trade Law: The GATT-WTO System, Regional Arrangements, and U.S. Law*, Charlottesville, VA: Lexis Law Publishing, 1998, pp. 527–28.

72. WTO, *Agreement on Subsidies and Countervailing Measures*, pp. 237–40, 260; U.S. House of Representatives, *Overview and Compilation*, p. 87.

73. This discussion of special and differential treatment draws on material from Peter Gallagher, *Guide to the WTO and Developing Countries*, Boston: Kluwer Law International, 2000, pp. 160–72 and Marc Benitah, *The Law of Subsidies under the GATT/WTO System*, New York: Kluwer Law International, 2001, pp. 37–44.

74. WTO, *Agreement on Subsidies and Countervailing Measures*, pp. 257–58.

75. It should be noted that due to a lack of clarity in the Uruguay Round Subsidies Agreement, the United States has continued to employ a less than 0.5 percent de minimis during its annual reviews of CVD decisions.

76. Article 17 of the Antidumping Agreement and Article 30 of the Subsidies Agreement refer WTO members to the dispute settlement system when conflicts arise. For more details, see WTO, *Agreement on Implementation of Article VI of the General Agreement on Tariffs and Trade 1994*, pp. 164–65; and WTO, *Understanding on Rules and Procedures Governing the Settlement of Disputes*, pp. 18–19 (available at www.wto.org/wto/dispute/dsu).

77. U.S. Department of Commerce, International Trade Administration, *Title VII of the Tariff Act of 1930, Updated through Public Law 103-465*, section 771(5); U.S. Department of Commerce, International Trade Administration, *Statement of Administrative Action*, *Agreement on Subsidies and Countervailing Measures*, pp. 2–3 (available from www.ita.doc.gov); U.S. Congress, *Uruguay Round Agreement Act*, p. 4922.

78. U.S. Department of Commerce, International Trade Administration, *Title VII of the Tariff Act of 1930 Update through Public Law 103-465*, sections 703 and 771(24)(B); U.S. Congress, *Uruguay Round Agreement Act*, p. 4915.

79. U.S. House of Representatives, *Overview and Compilation*, p. 106; U.S. Department of Commerce, International Trade Administration, *Title VII of the Tariff Act*

of 1930, Updated through Public Law 103-465, p. 49; U.S. Congress, *Uruguay Round Agreement Act*, title 1, subtitle c.

80. U.S. Congress, *Overview and Compilation*, p. 104.

81. Lande and Van Grasstek, *The Trade and Tariff Act of 1984*, pp. 111–15.

82. United States International Trade Commission, *The Year in Review: Fiscal Year 2000*, Washington, DC: USITC Publication, 2001, p. 82.

83. N. David Palmeter, "United States," in *Antidumping Under the WTO: A Comparative Review*, ed. Keith Steele, London: Kluwer Law International, 1996, p. 264.

~

Thailand's Antidumping and Countervailing Duty Problems

The purpose of this chapter is to examine the problems Thailand confronts as far as American antidumping (AD) and countervailing duty (CVD) actions are concerned. The discussion will focus on the types of cases that have been filed against Thailand since 1985, the results from those cases, and how the Thai government and two key Thai industries, the iron and steel and the pineapple canning industries, have responded to American actions. In addition, the results are reported from a survey that seeks to tap the perceptions Thai government officials and industry representatives have regarding United States and World Trade Organization (WTO) AD and CVD rules and procedures.

The discussion in this chapter is divided into four sections. The first examines Thailand's position in the world economy and as a trading partner of the United States. The second analyzes the types of AD and CVD cases that have been brought against Thai producers by the United States. The third describes the Thai government agencies that handle trade policy and the business groups that deal with the trade problems confronted by the iron and steel and pineapple industries. Finally, the last section reports interview results pertaining to the attitudes and perceptions that officials from government and industry have regarding American and WTO AD and CVD regulations.

Thailand's Trading Position

This section analyzes Thailand's position in world trade and as a partner of the United States. Table 3.1 displays Thailand's total exports and imports,

Table 3.1. Total Thai Exports and Imports, 1995–2000

	1995	1996	1997	1998	1999	2000
Total Exports	56,439	55,720	57,388	54,456	58,440	69,057
% of World Exports	1.11	1.04	1.04	1.00	1.03	1.09
Export Rank	21	23	23	23	22	23
Total Imports	70,786	72,331	62,853	42,971	50,342	61,924
% of World Imports	1.36	1.31	1.10	.96	.85	1.04
Import Rank	18	18	22	24	22	22

Note: Monetary values are in million United States dollars. Total trade figures and percentages are from the World Trade Organization, *International Trade Statistics*, 2001. Ranks are based on U.S. Department of Commerce, International Trade Administration, *U.S. Foreign Trade Highlights*, 2002.

the proportion of world exports and imports that result from Thai activity, and Thailand's rank in world trade. As can be seen from these data, since 1995 Thailand has consistently produced approximately 1 percent of world exports and has purchased nearly the same quantity of world production. During the same period, Thailand also has ranked as one of the top twenty-five nations in the world as far as both exports and imports are concerned. Among developing countries and regions, only Brazil, China, Hong Kong, Malaysia, Mexico, Saudi Arabia, and Singapore engage in more trade than Thailand.[1]

Clearly, Thailand is one of the world's most active participants in international commerce and is well positioned to play a leading role among developing countries. Additionally, as was noted in chapter 1, the substantial experience that these figures indicate Thailand has in world trade should make Thailand better equipped than most developing countries to handle trading problems and to understand the nuances of international trade regulations. If the results from the survey reported later in this chapter indicate that Thailand has difficulties with AD and CVD rules and procedures, then one can surmise that other developing countries most likely confront similar problems.

In addition to the role it plays in world trade, Thailand also has a large volume of trade with the United States. As table 3.2 shows, since 1995 the United States has ranked as Thailand's largest export market, absorbing between one-fifth and one-fourth of the goods Thailand sells to foreign countries. The United States is also the second largest source of Thailand's imports, accounting for approximately ten percent of the goods Thailand purchases abroad. Only Japan ranks ahead of the United States as a source of Thai imports.

From the American point of view, Thailand routinely ranks as one of the top fifteen sources of United States imports and as one of the twenty-six

Table 3.2. Total Thai Trade with the United States, 1995–2000

	1995	1996	1997	1998	1999	2000
Thai Exports to U.S.	11,348	11,336	12,602	13,436	14,330	16,385
% Thai Exports to U.S.	20.11	20.34	21.96	24.67	24.52	23.73
U.S. Rank as Thai Export Market	1	1	1	1	1	1
% U.S. Imports from Thailand	1.53	1.43	1.45	1.47	1.40	1.35
Thai Rank as a Source of U.S. Imports	13	14	14	13	13	15
Thai Imports from U.S.	6,665	7,198	7,349	5,239	4,985	6,618
% Thai Imports from U.S.	9.4	9.95	11.69	12.24	9.90	10.69
U.S. Rank as Source of Thai Imports	2	2	2	2	2	2
% U.S. Exports to Thailand	1.14	1.15	1.07	.77	.72	.85
Thai Rank as U.S. Export Market	18	20	21	26	25	22

Note: Monetary values are in million U.S. dollars. Data are from U.S. Department of Commerce, International Trade Administration, *U.S. Foreign Trade Highlights*, 2002, World Trade Organization, *International Trade Statistics*, 2001, and United Nations, *International Trade Statistics Yearbook*, 2000.

largest customers for United States exports. The only developing countries that rank ahead of Thailand as an American trading partner are Brazil, China, Korea, Malaysia, Mexico, Philippines, Singapore, Taiwan, and Venezuela.[2] As the figures for the percentage of United States imports and exports from Thailand indicate, however, the United States generally only sells about 1 percent of its exports to Thailand and buys only 1.5 percent of its imports from Thailand. A comparison of these figures with the same proportions for Thailand indicates just how asymmetrical the Thai-United States trading relationship is, for while the United States accounts for 20 to 25 percent of Thai exports and 10 to 12 percent of Thai imports, Thailand accounts for a much smaller proportion of United States imports and exports.

Thus, while Thailand and the United States play an important role in each other's international commercial activities, the United States clearly is the senior partner in the relationship. It should be noted that many international analysts regard such disparities in the level of trade as one finds in the United States-Thai relationship as a potential source of power that may permit the larger partner to dominate the smaller.[3] In part, this domination usually is attributed to the relative ease with which the smaller state can be replaced as a source of imports and as a market for exports as compared to the more insurmountable problems associated with finding a replacement for the markets and goods of the larger state. Based on these figures, one might tentatively conclude that Thai representatives would hesitate to challenge American trade moves due to the fear that such challenges would imperil their relations with a dominant trading partner. The interview data reported later in this chapter will offer an opportunity to assess this preliminary conclusion.

United States AD and CVD Cases against Thailand

Having presented an initial picture of Thailand's international trading position and of its relationship with the United States, attention can now turn to an examination of the Thai experience as a target of United States AD and CVD cases. The first Thai experience with American AD and CVD regulations came in 1984 when the United States conducted an investigation of the subsidies provided to the Thai textile industry. In that case, the Thai government was able to avoid the imposition of duties by terminating some of the subsidies in question and by altering several others to the satisfaction of

Table 3.3. United States Antidumping Cases against Thailand, 1985–2001

Year	Number Filed	Number of Cases with Duties	Industry
1985	1	1	Steel
1986	1	1	Steel
1987	0	0	
1988	1	1	Bearings
1989	0	0	
1990	1	0	Steel
1991	1	1	Steel
1992	0	0	
1993	1	0	Pencils
1994	4	2	Steel (n), Lighters (n), Alcohol (y), Pineapples (y)
1995	0	0	
1996	0	0	
1997	0	0	
1998	0	0	
1999	1	0	Steel
2000	1	0	Steel
2001	1	1	Steel

Total Cases: 13   % Cases with Duties: 54

Sources: U.S. International Trade Commission, *Antidumping and Countervailing Orders in Place as of April 25, 2002*, by Countries, and U.S. Department of Commerce, International Trade Administration, *AD and CVD Investigations Decisions*, 2000.

the United States. Hence, this initial CVD investigation did not result in American action against Thai textile exports.[4]

Complaints from American producers against Thai corporate and government practices continued throughout the 1980s and 1990s and resulted in the imposition in 1985 of the first AD and CVD duties against Thai products. As tables 3.3 and 3.4 show, in the years between 1985 and 2001, Thai producers were the target of thirteen antidumping investigations and ten countervailing duty complaints. Among developing countries, only Argentina, Brazil, China, India, Korea, Mexico, Taiwan, and Venezuela have been subjected to more investigations.[5]

As far as its AD cases are concerned, table 3.3 shows that seven of the thirteen investigations of Thai corporations that have been conducted by the United States have resulted in the imposition of duties. This means that 54 percent of the AD cases that have been brought have had adverse findings from the Thai point of view. While the number of CVD filings have been fewer than the number of AD filings, table 3.4 indicates that the rate at which duties have been imposed has been greater. Of the ten CVD cases that

Table 3.4. United States Countervailing Duty Cases against Thailand, 1985–2001

Year	Number Filed	Number of Cases with Duties	Industry
1985	2	2	Steel, Rice
1986	0	0	
1987	1	1	Steel
1988	2	2	Bearings, Steel
1989	1	1	Steel
1990	1	1	Steel
1991	0	0	
1992	0	0	
1993	0	0	
1994	1	0	Lighters
1995	0	0	
1996	0	0	
1997	0	0	
1998	0	0	
1999	1	0	Steel
2000	0	0	
2001	1	1	Steel

Total Cases: 10   % Cases with Duties: 80

Sources: U.S. International Trade Commission, *Antidumping and Countervailing Duties in Place as of April 25, 2002, by Country,* and U.S. Department of Commerce, International Trade Administration, *AD and CVD Investigations Decisions,* 2001.

have investigated Thai subsidies, eight have resulted in duties. That is, 80 percent of the CVD cases have led to findings against Thailand.

It is interesting to consider the Thai industries that have been the target of American AD and CVD complaints. Of the thirteen AD filings since 1985, table 3.3 shows that eight have been aimed at some part of the steel industry. This is 62 percent of the total. In addition to steel, single cases were filed against the ball bearings, pencil, cigarette lighter, alcohol, and pineapple industries. The steel industry also has played a prominent role in CVD cases, for, as table 3.4 indicates, seven of the ten CVD filings since 1985 have involved some part of the steel industry. This is 70 percent of the total. Other industries targeted by CVD complaints have included rice, ball bearings, and cigarette lighters.

These findings for Thailand conform to the broader picture of how AD and CVD cases are used both in the United States and around the world. As Marvel and Ray note, the steel industry accounts for the majority of AD and CVD filings in the United States. Destler makes a similar point, and World Trade Organization statistics show that the steel industry plays a prominent part in unfair trade investigations worldwide. Indeed, WTO figures show that between 1995 and 2002 steel cases out number those for any other industry when one considers the global AD filings, while steel CVD cases outnumber those for all other industries combined. Therefore, one can draw the preliminary conclusion that the Thai experience with American AD and CVD rules and procedures mirrors the experiences of many other countries.[6]

Having examined the Thai position in international commerce, as a trading partner with the United States, and as far as American AD and CVD investigations are concerned, attention can now turn to the examination of how Thailand handles the AD and CVD cases that are filed against Thai producers. This task is the subject of the remainder of this chapter. In the next section, the discussion will focus on how the government and private industry are organized in Thailand. Following this, the results from interviews with governmental officials and industry representatives are presented.

The Organization of Thai Government and Industry

The Thai Government

In order to investigate the Thai reaction to United States AD and CVD actions, one must first describe both the Thai government agencies that handle trade-related problems and the industry organizations that are responsible for working with the government on issues pertaining to trade. This section performs those tasks. To begin with the government, Thailand is organized as a constitutional monarchy with an elected National Assembly that has two houses, the House of Representatives and the Senate. The Head of the Thai government, or Prime Minister, is selected by majority vote of the House of Representatives. Since Thailand has a multiparty system, the Prime Minister must usually put together and maintain a coalition of several political parties in order to obtain the votes needed for election to office. In a departure from the typical parliamentary style of government, the Prime Minister and the ministers selected to head the various cabinet-level agencies within the Thai government do not sit in the House of Representatives or in the Senate. Instead, the Prime Minister serves as the head of the executive branch and ministers are picked from among prominent academics, business people, lawyers, politicians, and so forth.

Within the Thai government, three agencies play a dominant role in trade policy: (1) the Ministry of Commerce, (2) the Office of the Board of Investment, and (3) the Bank of Thailand. The Ministry of Commerce is a cabinet-level agency that is responsible for handling the problems Thai businesses confront, both domestically and internationally. Within the Ministry of Commerce, the Department of Foreign Trade and the Department of Trade Negotiation (formerly the Department of Business Economics) play predominant parts in the trade policy process, and within these Departments the Bureau of Trade Interests and Remedies and the Bureau of Multilateral Trade Negotiations are responsible for working on matters relating to antidumping and countervailing duty actions.

The Bureau of Trade Interests and Remedies (BTIR) is a part of the Department of Foreign Trade. The BTIR consists of seven divisions: (1) the General Administrative Section, (2) the Regulation Group, (3) the AD/CVD Defense Group, (4) the Investigation Group, (5) the Injury Investigation Group, (6) the Safeguard Group, and (7) the Public Affairs Section. In the area of AD and CVD actions, the BTIR assists with Thai AD and CVD investigations, studies and analyzes the AD and CVD regulations and acts of other countries, considers the effects on the Thai economy of foreign AD and CVD behavior, and assists Thai businesses as they respond to AD and CVD problems.[7]

The Bureau of Multilateral Trade Negotiations (BMTN) is part of the Department of Trade Negotiation. As far as AD and CVD issues are concerned, the BMTN is responsible for developing Thai negotiating positions at the WTO, at Association of Southeast Asian Nations (ASEAN) meetings, at Asia Pacific Economic Cooperation (APEC) meetings, and in other international bargaining sessions. The BMTN also monitors the WTO dispute settlement process regarding matters pertaining to ADs and CVDs and plays a role in resolving bilateral disputes relating to ADs and CVDs when and if the matter is referred to the WTO.[8]

The Office of the Board of Investment (BOI) is the second government agency that plays a prominent part in handling unfair trade matters for Thailand. The BOI is housed within the Office of the Prime Minister and is chaired by the Prime Minister. The BOI is responsible for encouraging domestic and foreign investments that stimulate the Thai economy and promote economic growth and development. The BOI also assists Thai firms when they invest abroad and seeks to increase Thailand's industrial and technological capabilities. The BOI has the additional responsibility of aiding Thai corporations that face foreign CVD investigations, but plays no role in the AD process.[9]

The final governmental agency that deals with unfair trade is the Bank of Thailand (BOT). The BOT was set up as an independent government agency in 1942. The BOT funds the Thai Export-Import Bank, promotes Thai research and development activities, and manages the Thai banking system in much the same way that the Federal Reserve handles the American banking system. As far as unfair trade is concerned, the BOT plays a role that is similar to the BOI, for it assists Thai firms that face foreign CVD actions.[10]

Private Industry in Thailand

Having described the key governmental agencies that handle matters pertaining to ADs and CVDs, attention can now turn to the private industry groups that play a role in the process. As was noted in chapter 1, the industries examined in this research are those that produce steel and canned pineapples. The steel industry was selected because of the exceedingly prominent role it has as a target of American AD and CVD cases. The pineapple industry is included in the analysis because it has faced far fewer AD and CVD cases and can be compared to steel to determine how the frequency of complaints affects perceptions. In addition, pineapples are examined to determine whether the AD and CVD problems affecting a heavy industry that faces the intense international competition confronted by steel also affect a food-oriented business that exports a large part of its production.

The private sector in Thailand is organized on a cooperative basis with the government. Instead of practicing the interest group style pressuring tactics that are common in the United States, private interests in Thailand tend to make their voices heard by participating in committees and organizations that bring private and public groups together to discuss the issues that are of concern to both.

As far as trade is concerned, the largest and most influential committee is the Joint WTO Committee on Commerce, Industry, and Banking of Thailand (the Joint WTO Committee). The Joint WTO Committee was established in 1999 and includes as members the Board of Trade of Thailand, the Federation of Thai Industries (described below), and the Thai Bankers' Association. The primary purposes of the Joint WTO Committee are to aid the government as it develops the Thai bargaining position for WTO negotiations, to help the private sector adjust as the Thai economy becomes more open to international commerce, and to serve as a vehicle for bringing the trade-related complaints of Thai businesses to the attention of the government. In the area of ADs and CVDs, the Joint WTO committee is one of the primary means by which the government is informed of the various problems Thai exporters have when they confront foreign unfair trade investigations.[11]

A second influential Thai organization is the Federation of Thai Industries (FTI). The FTI was set up in 1987 as a reorganized version of the twenty-year-old Association of Thai Industries. The FTI is an umbrella organization that includes twenty-eight industry clubs from four product groups: (1) commodities, (2) industry, (3) raw materials, and (4) consumer goods. The Thai Iron and Steel Industry Club and the Thai Food Processors' Association (also referred to as the Thai Food Processors' Club) belong to the FTI. The FTI serves as a focal point for channeling information to the government regarding the needs of its various members. The most important means by which this information reaches the government is through the role the FTI plays on the Joint Public-Private Sector Consultative Committee, which is headed by the Prime Minister. The FTI's role concerning ADs and CVDs includes: (1) coordinating industry complaints, (2) advising individual corporations about the problems that can stem from ADs and CVDs, and (3) analyzing the effects AD and CVD actions have on Thai businesses.[12]

As mentioned above, the FTI includes as a member the Thai Iron and Steel Industry Club (TISIC). The TISIC was set up in 1978. It includes 104 members from among the businesses that produce iron and steel products in Thailand. The TISIC's primary functions are to monitor the quality of Thai iron and steel products, to coordinate research and development for the industry, to promote trade, and to encourage greater levels of cooperation among iron and steel producers throughout Southeast Asia. In addition, the TISIC plays a major role in assisting Thai corporations when they face AD and CVD investigations, acts as an industry coordinator both when handling foreign AD and CVD investigations and when discussing the proper strategy to employ to avoid foreign AD and CVD complaints, and brings industry AD and CVD concerns to the attention of the Thai government.[13]

The Thai Food Processors' Association (TFPA) is also a member of the Federation of Thai Industries. The TFPA was created in 1970 and includes 106 food packing companies and 80 food trading firms as its members. The food packing members are divided into four groups: (1) the pineapple packers group, (2) the fruit and vegetable packers group, (3) the tuna packers group, and (4) the seafood packers group. The TFPA promotes quality control, information exchanges among food processors, assists businesses facing AD and CVD actions, organizes legal appeals regarding foreign AD and CVD measures, and ensures that the government is aware of member concerns regarding foreign AD and CVD regulations.[14]

As was just mentioned, the Thai Pineapple Packers Group (TPPG) forms one of the divisions within the Thai Food Processors' Association. The TPPG is comprised of twenty-four pineapple-packing firms that engage in exporting. The TPPG is the front line organization for handling the trade problems confronted by its member firms. Regarding unfair trade, the TPPG focuses its attention on assisting corporations that confront foreign AD complaints. The assistance provided includes advice regarding how to respond to foreign inquiries and help in locating foreign legal representation and in negotiating with other governments.[15]

To summarize the material presented above, the most important private industry participants in handling the unfair trade problems of the iron and steel and pineapple packing industries in Thailand are the Joint WTO Committee, the Federation of Thai Industries, the Thai Iron and Steel Industry Club, the Thai Food Processors' Association, and the Thai Pineapple Packers Group. As will be described below, representatives from these groups were interviewed in order to obtain information regarding the problems private corporations in Thailand confront when they face foreign AD and CVD investigations.

Interview Results

As was mentioned in chapter 1, interviews were conducted with personnel from each of the trade-related organizations described in the previous section of this chapter. These interviews took place in June and July of 2000. Follow-up interviews were conducted between May and June of 2005. For the most part, the results from the two sets of interviews were the same. Hence, distinctions between the 2000 and 2005 interviews are made only when there are significant differences to report. The questionnaire that was used to organize the interviews may be found in Appendix B. As was mentioned in chapter 1, all interviews were conducted in Thai, which is the native language of one of the authors.

To summarize the survey briefly, it should be noted that it included questions designed to tap nine types of issues and problems confronted by the Thai government and Thai industry pertaining to the AD and CVD investigations conducted by the United States as far as Thailand is concerned. The issues and problems included those relating to: (1) knowledge, (2) procedures, (3) cooperation, (4) assistance, (5) burdens, (6) settlement, (7) retaliation and appeals, (8) negotiations, and (9) impact.

From the outset, it should be mentioned that several respondents hesitated to answer questions, citing the sensitive nature of the issue because trade is one of the most important of Thailand's national interests. For the most part, those who responded in this way expressed the concern that their answers might provide the United States and other Thai trading partners with an advantage in the highly competitive world of international commerce. Some interviewees also were apprehensive that Thai comments might lead foreign governments to believe that the Thai government was engaging in trade practices that violate WTO rules. In other cases, selected questions were omitted from interviews because they were beyond the field of specialization of the agency a respondent represented.

For interviewees expressing concerns about Thai national interests, the interview procedure was adjusted to allow the respondents to make a statement regarding the information they were prepared to share with the researcher. These statements were made after the interviewee had examined the questionnaire and had discussed with the researcher the types of information that were sought. Therefore, those making statements received guidance from the researcher that encouraged them to provide as much of the desired information as possible.

For reasons of confidentiality, the names of the individuals who were interviewed are not disclosed. Instead, the interviewees are identified by the title they hold within the organization they serve. All respondents were told that this method would be used for noting who had participated in the survey. Everyone stated that they were comfortable with this procedure.[16]

Among the government agencies examined, the following people were interviewed:

1. Bureau of Trade Interests and Remedies—The Director of the Bureau and the Assistant Director in charge of the United States and European Antidumping and Countervailing Section,
2. Bureau of Multilateral Trade Negotiations—A Senior Expert in Multilateral Trade,
3. Board of Investment—A Senior Expert in the International Affairs Division and a Senior Official on International Affairs, and

4. Bank of Thailand—An Official in the Financial Market Operation Group and an Official in the Monetary Policy Group.

In private industry, the interviewees included:

1. Joint WTO Committee—The Chair of the Subcommittee on Law and Investment,
2. Federation of Thai Industries—A member of the Executive Committee,
3. Thai Iron and Steel Industry Club—The Deputy Secretary General,
4. Thai Food Processors' Association—The Vice-Chairman for International Trade and the Deputy Manager for International Trade, and
5. Thai Pineapple Packers Group—The Chairwoman for the Group.

The results of the interviews are organized according to issue. Hence, the knowledge-related answers from the government and private industry respondents are discussed first, followed in turn by answers pertaining to the questions about procedures, cooperation, assistance, burdens, and so forth. Following the presentation of the results, the implications for United States–Thai trade relations are considered.

Knowledge Issues
The knowledge questions deal with the degree to which respondents feel that the Thai government and Thai corporations employ enough specialists who understand United States and WTO AD and CVD rules and procedures. Beyond this, the questions seek to determine how Thai specialists obtain their training and whether the United States and the WTO provide assistance in that area. Among government interviewees, only the officials from the Bureau of Trade Interests and Remedies (BTIR) answered these questions. From the private sector, only the representative from the Thai Iron and Steel Industry Club (TISIC) responded to all of the questions, while the respondents from the Thai Food Processors' Association (TFPA), the Federation of Thai Industries (FTI), and the Joint WTO Committee addressed selected questions.

Beginning with the government officials, there was a general feeling that the BTIR does not have the expertise needed to handle United States and WTO AD and CVD cases. Indeed, one of the interviewees stated that Thai corporations often had a greater level of knowledge in this area than did the BTIR. These officials also stated that both the government and private companies rely very heavily on the advice they receive from United States trade lawyers when dealing with American investigations, but stated that they felt comfortable when doing so because these attorneys appeared to do a good job representing Thai interests. As far as training is concerned, the BTIR representatives said that such training was difficult to acquire in Thailand because of tight budgets and difficulties relating to the fact that many trade rules are in English. As a result, the Thai government depends upon American trade lawyers for educational efforts. Finally, it was noted that while the WTO provides some training assistance regarding WTO rules, the aid that is given is far too general and does little to help local officials understand technical details.

From among the private industry respondents, the TISIC representative agreed with many of the comments made by the BTIR officials. It was noted that Thai organizations, both governmental and private, do not have enough specialists who understand United States and WTO AD and CVD regulations. The TISIC interviewee also stated that Thai companies depend on American trade attorneys to represent their interests and expressed satisfaction with the efforts these lawyers make on behalf of Thai corporations. It was noted that American attorneys also frequently train the employees of Thai firms and that much of this training is obtained on a voluntary basis wherein interested employees sought out United States lawyers for assistance.

A slightly conflicting view of American attorneys emerged during the 2005 interview with the Thai Pineapple Packers Group (TPPG) representative. This respondent noted that while foreign lawyers usually did an excellent job for Thai pineapple corporations, in 2003 it had been necessary for one pineapple company to terminate relations with a Washington law firm because it failed to handle a case properly. Hence, while American attorneys generally were given high praise for the jobs they did, there was at least one instance in which they did not perform as expected.

Regarding foreign assistance in educating the Thais, the TISIC respondent gave the United States International Trade Commission and the WTO credit for sending specialists to Thailand to provide training for Thai corporate representatives. It was noted, however, that many of the seminars that were held early on were too vague because they did not provide details about how AD and CVD inquiries were conducted and did not elaborate on how decisions are made during American investigations. The 2005 follow-up interview indicated that by 2002 the WTO training sessions were much better. In fact, the TISIC respondent stated that a WTO seminar in 2002 was especially valuable for providing information about United States AD rules and procedures.

Finally, the TISIC representative stated that although most of the companies in the iron and steel group did not have a proper knowledge of how the WTO handles AD and CVD cases, TISIC was making efforts to correct that deficiency. Such knowledge was regarded as essential to ensure that Thai companies did not mistakenly violate unfair trade laws and to guarantee that companies would understand their options if they faced a foreign unfair trade case. Along those same lines, the respondents from the FTI and the Joint WTO Committee agreed that Thai companies need to learn more about how the WTO operates if they are to protect their interests in international commerce.

Interestingly, the representative from the TFPA had a completely different view about acquiring knowledge about the WTO, stating that such information was not especially important and could be provided by trade lawyers if and when it was required. One might speculate that this divergence of opinion about the WTO can be traced to the frequency with which an industry has faced AD and CVD cases. As noted earlier in this chapter, the iron and steel industry (which the TISIC represents) has faced many such cases over the years, both in the United States and internationally, while the food processing industry (which the TFPA represents) has faced only one case (pineapples in 1994) in the United States and three additional cases from the rest of the world. The other cases involved canned tomatoes in 1991 and canned tuna and canned pineapples in 2001, all brought by Australia.[17] Therefore, one might expect the steel industry to feel a more urgent need to become acquainted with national and international AD and CVD regulations than would the canned pineapple industry. It should be recalled that the TISIC is affiliated directly with the FTI and indirectly (through the FTI) with the Joint WTO Committee, which may explain the interest those organizations have in WTO rules.

Procedural Questions
The procedural part of the questionnaire taps the degree to which respondents understand the methods the United States employs when conducting AD and CVD investigations. In particular, this section seeks to determine whether the Thais are comfortable with the way the United States conducts its investigations, whether the United States follows WTO rules regarding AD and CVD cases, how well the Thais understand the timetables and information gathering techniques used during investigations, and whether the Thais feel that American procedures are sufficiently transparent.

Among governmental respondents, the two interviewees from the Bureau of Trade Interests and Remedies (BTIR) were the only officials to address this group of questions. When asked about their comfort level with American procedures, these officials stated that while the United States generally follows WTO rules during AD and CVD cases, American investigators often did not understand Thai confidentiality laws. As a result, the United States Department of Commerce (DOC) frequently seemed to believe that Thai government agencies should provide the DOC with information even when doing so might be illegal under Thai law.

Private industry respondents from the Thai Iron and Steel Industry Club (TISIC), the Thai Food Processors' Association (TFPA), and the Thai Pineapple Packers Group (TPPG) offered a somewhat different picture of American procedures, arguing that the questions included on DOC AD surveys often were designed to trick Thai corporations, were so complex that it was nearly impossible to provide an appropriate answer, and sometimes appeared to require the disclosure of business secrets that would harm corporate competitiveness in international commerce. In addition, the TISIC, the TFPA, and the TPPG representatives expressed considerable discomfort with what they considered the excessively brief amounts of time for filling out questionnaires that American procedures gave to foreign businesses under investigation. The TPPG respondent also noted that American practices discriminated against small firms. Such firms were seen as being at a disadvantage because they could not afford to hire an attorney in the United States to assist in filling out the DOC questionnaire and defending their cases.

Both the government respondents from the BTIR and the private interviewees from the TISIC and the TFPA agreed that the United States conforms to WTO rules when conducting its investigations. These respondents also stated that they were personally aware that American law provides for the use of the "best information available" (BIA, see chapter 2) when the target of an investigation does not provide an adequate response and that this information may be obtained from a competing American company. However, each person interviewed considered these procedures unfair, and the private industry representatives noted that inexperienced and smaller Thai companies often did not realize the circumstances under which BIA might be used and what the consequences might be.

In the 2005 interviews, the TPPG respondent asserted that Thai pineapple companies have found that the United States sometimes takes a questionable approach to WTO rules. Of particular concern were American practices regarding the de minimis levels employed during annual and sunset reviews (see chapter 2, footnote 75) and the practice of zeroing. Zeroing involves setting negative dumping margins (a higher foreign than domestic price) to zero when averaging to determine whether dumping has occurred during a given time period.[18] The TPPG noted both that zeroing greatly increases the probability that a company will be found guilty of dumping and that in its opinion WTO rules forbid the practice. Nonetheless, the TPPG argued that the DOC continues to employ zeroing.

In discussing United States timetables, the TISIC and TFPA respondents noted that while the period allowed for filling out DOC questionnaires was unfairly brief, the overall amount of time devoted to an investigation was far too long.[19] This last concern was a product of the fact that Thai corporations usually found it difficult to sell in the American market while they were under investigation. Additional comments about timetables came from the TPPG interviewee, who complained that the brief period for completing questionnaires severely hampers Thai companies with foreign affiliations because foreign affiliates often could not supply data quickly enough to conform to what the DOC expected. Reference was made to a 2002 pineapple case in which the DOC employed the best information available because a Thai company was unable to obtain timely data from a Japanese affiliate.

Officials from the BTIR noted during the 2005 interviews that the Thai government and private industry have adopted a new practice for handling the strict American timetables. This method involves retaining attorneys in Washington to monitor AD and CVD cases and to warn the Thais whenever an action against a Thai firm is imminent. In this way, Thai authorities are able to move quickly to begin preparing their response to the American complaint. Of course, the down side to the new system is the high cost of lawyers, who must be paid a retainer to provide the monitoring service.

Finally, as far as transparency is concerned, government and private industry interviewees alike claimed that United States rules and procedures were so complex as to impede transparency and that the DOC made little effort to explain how and why decisions were made. In fact, the TISIC respondent referred to DOC procedures as being conducted within a "black box" that was designed to obscure what was going on inside. Under these conditions, the Thais felt that they were placed at such an extreme disadvantage that it was nearly impossible to abide by American rules even when they made an effort to do so.

Cooperation Issues

This group of questions examined the degree to which the Thai government and Thai corporations willingly supplied American AD and CVD investigators with the information required for their investigations. Starting with the issue of governmental cooperation, the officials interviewed at each of the governmental agencies included in the survey indicated that the Thai government cooperates as much as possible with United States investigations. It was stated that the government's willingness to cooperate is a product of the awareness that refusals to supply data will not halt American investigations, but instead will lead the United States Department of Commerce (DOC) to resort to the use of the best information available (BIA). Each of the governmental interviewees expressed the concern that an American use of BIA would lead to an outcome that would damage Thai interests far more than would be the case if the Thais provided the requested information. In fact, the respondent from the Thai Board of Investment (BOI) went so far as to assert that cooperating with American investigators was in the Thai national interest because it was only through such cooperation that the Thais could receive the lowest possible CVD duties and that such low duties were essential in order for Thailand to maintain the export levels needed to promote economic growth and development.

Even though the government officials all expressed an interest in cooperation, several stated that they had reservations about the American investigatory process. Officials from the Bureau of Trade Interests and Remedies (BTIR) indicated that they felt that United States investigators do not show a proper respect for Thai sovereignty and that DOC representatives sometimes reject the data provided by the Thai government, claiming that the data are inappropriate or inaccurate.

The Bank of Thailand (BOT) interviewees offered another complaint, pointing out that on occasion American investigators are heavy-handed in their data gathering techniques in that they demand information pertaining to several Thai companies even if the focal point for their inquiries is a single Thai firm. The BOT noted that when this occurs, the Thais usually provide the information requested by the DOC in order to avoid the use of BIA, which as was mentioned above, is universally regarded as leading to extremely adverse consequences. Nonetheless, the BOT indicated that American data demands can lead to misunderstandings between the Thai government and Thai companies. One example of such trouble is when firms resent having what they regard as confidential information provided to the DOC. A BTIR official pointed out that another problem can result if a company gets a high CVD rate and feels that the rate is a product of a lack of proper cooperation on the part of the BOT. Indeed, the Thai Iron and Steel Industry Club (TISIC) representative complained that in the recent past a lack of BOT cooperation in providing data for a Canadian CVD investigation had led to a high CVD duty for a Thai steel corporation. Apparently, the BOT is now going to great lengths to avoid a repetition of the Canadian case.

As far as corporate cooperation is concerned, the BTIR interviewees stated that the government openly encourages Thai companies to provide American investigations with whatever data they request. The BTIR noted that the government works especially closely with Thai companies during DOC on-the-spot investigations (also referred to in the United States as verification investigations) in Thailand. During this phase of the DOC investigation, the BTIR officials stated that their agency routinely holds meetings with the affected corporations in an effort to ensure that DOC questions are answered in a prompt and relevant fashion.

From the corporate point of view, the TISIC and the Thai Food Processors' Association (TFPA) representatives noted that private industry cooperation with DOC investigations was a product of corporate experience with unfair trade complaints. Companies that have been targets of such cases in the past were labeled as far more likely to cooperate than those that have not. Inexperienced companies were described as less cooperative because they feared the revelation of trade secrets and other sensitive information. The Thai Pineapple Packers Group (TPPG) representative noted that, as far as trade was concerned, one of its most important services to its member companies involved alerting them to the need to avoid BIA by cooperating with foreign AD investigations.

Finally, the BTIR officials explained that three factors were important determinants of when a Thai company cooperated with an American investigation. The first was whether the company considered the requested data confidential. The second was whether the Thai company was a part of a joint venture with a foreign firm that did not wish to cooperate in an investigation. It was explained that on occasion foreign firms worried that cooperation would lead to the revelation of trade secrets. The third had to do with whether a Thai company would face complications with the Thai Customs Service if its import and export activities received close scrutiny. In the absence of these types of problems, the BTIR stated that Thai companies usually do all they can to assist the DOC with its investigations. Once, again, the motive for this willingness to cooperate was the desire to avoid the use of BIA by the DOC.

Assistance Issues
This collection of questions deals with how the Thai government aids Thai firms with the problems they confront due to American AD and CVD actions. In particular, the inquiries dealt with whether the Thai government helps Thai corporations: (1) understand United States and WTO AD and CVD rules, (2) locate legal assistance in the United States, (3) fill out the complex forms that the United States employs when conducting investiga-

tions, and (4) provides funds to defray the costs Thai firms incur when they are investigated.

Beginning with the questions relating to understanding United States and WTO rules, the officials from the Bureau of Trade Interests and Remedies (BTIR) stated that their agency provides assistance in this area by organizing seminars and lectures for private industry at which American trade lawyers and representatives from the WTO appear. In addition, the BTIR helps Thai companies by translating WTO documents from English into Thai. The interviewee from the Thai Iron and Steel Industry Club (TISIC) noted that such educational efforts do exist, but as was mentioned above, expressed concern that they often did not provide enough details to be of value. In addition, the TISIC representative claimed that unless Thai companies had been the targets of foreign AD and CVD cases they had little interest in attending seminars and lectures because they did not fully appreciate the importance of United States and WTO rules. The Thai Food Processors' Association (TFPA) respondents agreed with the above and added that governmental educational programs were of recent origin, especially in the area of ADs, because previously there had been an attitude on the part of the government that companies facing dumping investigations should be faulted for not exercising more care in the conduct of their export business. However, as the number of foreign AD cases has increased over time, the TFPA representative noted that the government has become more active in educational efforts because of the mounting damage to the volume of Thai exports.

The next questions focused on legal representation. The interviewees at the BTIR claimed that the government is always ready to help Thai firms find attorneys when they request such assistance, and the TISIC and TFPA representatives agreed that such aid was available. As far as paying the costs associated with hiring attorneys was concerned, the BTIR official said that the procedure normally employed was for private firms to pay when they faced AD investigations and for the government to pay for CVD cases. The TISIC and the TFPA representatives agreed that this was the standard practice. The BTIR officials noted, however, that a special exception has been made for the canned pineapple industry since that industry is of such widespread importance to Thai farmers and because the industry has had such limited experience with AD complaints in the past. In the case of canned pineapple, it was stated that there has been a fund to help defray some of the costs associated with hiring attorneys for AD cases. It was explained that these funds were limited, were only meant to be available for two cases, and that this assistance would be phased out as the industry gained experience in handling AD complaints.[20]

Finally, all respondents were asked about whether the government helps Thai firms fill out the voluminous forms used in AD and CVD cases. The BTIR officials explained that at first the normal practice was for private companies to handle AD forms and to send copies to the BTIR, while the government took care of CVD forms. By 2005, however, the BTIR representatives stated that special workshops are now held for firms facing foreign unfair trade complaints. These workshops were set up in response to private industry calls for help and to ensure that strict foreign timetables would be met and that the proper information would be provided to investigators. The TFPA and the TISIC interviewees agreed with the picture presented by the BTIR.

Burden Questions

These questions deal with the costs Thai companies incur when they face AD and CVD investigations. The focus is on the specific nature of those costs and on whether the initiation of unfair trade investigations leads to the loss of business in the United States.

Starting with the nature of the costs, the Bureau of Trade Interests and Remedies (BTIR), the Bureau of Multilateral Trade Negotiations (BMTN), the Thai Iron and Steel Industry Club (TISIC), and the Thai Food Processors' Association (TFPA) interviewees all stated that the primary costs were the immense time required for handling an investigation, the large number of personnel needed to deal with cases, and the expenses associated with hiring United States attorneys. The BMTN respondent noted that American CVD investigations sometimes took a "shot-gun" approach, sending lengthy questionnaires to any Thai government agency that was suspected of offering a trade subsidy, and pointed out that handling inquiries of this type was extremely costly to the affected governmental agencies. The BTIR representatives estimated the average initial cost of an attorney for a CVD case at over $150,000, while the private industry respondents said that attorneys for an AD case usually cost at least $250,000. For both types of investigations, it was noted that legal defense costs often were much higher. The TISIC and TFPA representatives noted that such attorney's fees often were beyond the amount that smaller companies could afford and argued that as a result some companies were unable to contest the unfair trade cases they confronted.

Regarding the issue of losing business due to an unfair trade case, all respondents, both governmental and private, claimed that AD and CVD investigations led to lost sales. The BTIR stated that smaller Thai firms frequently lost business because they simply abandoned the American market if they received an adverse unfair trade ruling. The TISIC and the TFPA representatives agreed and added that Thai firms that were under the cloud of an unfair trade investigation sometimes found that American importers would switch their business either to foreign firms that did not face investigations, to Thai firms that have joint ventures with United States corporations, to Thai or other foreign firms that face lower AD and CVD rates, or to domestic American firms. As a result, the private industry respondents felt that the burdens associated with AD and CVD cases often were immense and frequently had devastating consequences for Thai corporations.

Settlement Issues
This section of the questionnaire examined issues relating to: (1) whether Thai companies were inclined to seek an agreement whereby American unfair trade investigations would be terminated or suspended in return for self-imposed limitations on the amount of their exports to the United States and (2) the degree to which Thai firms felt that American corporations used AD and CVD investigations to harass their Thai competitors. In their response to these questions, the government officials from the Bureau of Trade Interests and Remedies (BTIR) said that they were unable to comment on how Thai firms might choose to handle AD cases, but that when it came to CVDs, the government was hesitant to request that investigations be suspended. The BTIR respondents explained that the government usually avoided suspensions due to the fear that the concessions required to obtain a suspension would result in more severe limitations on Thai trade than would such duties as might be applied if an investigations led to an adverse finding. The Board of Investment (BOI) official added that under Thai law it is not possible to negotiate suspension agreements that involve the termination of subsidies because Thai law states that subsidies can only be stopped if the recipient company requests that they be ended. Hence, the government has little flexibility when it comes to agreements of this sort.

The private industry representatives from the Thai Iron and Steel Industry Club (TISIC) and the Thai Food Processors' Association (TFPA) voiced concerns about suspensions that paralleled those expressed by the BTIR interviewees. In each case, the industry respondents indicated a dislike of suspensions due to the fear that suspensions would lead to quotas that would be more trade restrictive than any possible AD or CVD duties. Instead, they mentioned that the preferred strategy was to see investigations through to their conclusion and to do everything possible to ensure that any AD and CVD rates that might be imposed would be as low as possible.

As far as the question of harassment is concerned, only the representatives from the TISIC and the TFPA offered a response. In each case, the interviewees indicated that they strongly agreed with the contention that their United States competitors use unfair trade allegations as a form of harassment. The TFPA respondent stated that the inconveniences associated with investigations went beyond the problems relating to fighting the case to include the need to monitor pricing in third country markets and production costs in both the United States and Thailand. By way of explanation, the TFPA representative noted that third country sales sometimes were used when calculating dumping margins and that the changing costs of production inputs often brought dumping complaints in the United States. That is, the fear was expressed that if production costs went down, the result might be dumping complaints in the United States because Thai canned pineapples might undercut the cost of American grown pineapples. Likewise, if United States prices increase, then American firms might target lower cost Thai canned pineapple for a complaint. Monitoring production and costs in so many markets was described as expensive and as leading to problems for Thai companies.

In the 2005 follow-up, the TISIC interviewees claimed that some Thai steel companies had recently experienced a new form of harassment in which an American firm filed a dumping complaint with the United States Commerce Department and later withdrew the case after the Thai firm named in the complaint had incurred the expenses associated with hiring attorneys to respond. It was stated that one corporate member of TISIC had run up over $200,000 in legal expenses due to such a move by an American steel company. Quite naturally, the Thais resent such behavior and regard it as an indication that United States unfair trade rules are themselves unfair and allow American firms to torment their foreign competitors.

Retaliation and Appeal

This part of the interview attempted to tap the degree to which the Thais retaliate against the United States over American AD and CVD actions and/or appeal American decisions either to United States courts or to the WTO. When evaluating the question of retaliation, two types of behavior were considered: (1) imposing AD and/or CVD duties against United States exports to Thailand and (2) taking positions at the WTO or in other international settings that opposed the American position. The governmental respondents to the retaliation questions were from the Bureau of Trade Interests and Remedies (BTIR), while the private industry respondents were from the Federation of Thai Industries (FTI) and from the Joint WTO Committee.

Starting with the question of imposing duties to counter American AD and/or CVD actions, the officials from the government stated that the Thais do not engage in such behavior. It was explained that such retaliation is nearly impossible because Thai AD and CVD laws set specific standards for conducting AD and CVD investigations and that unless those criteria are met no action can be taken. In other words, the government cannot simply initiate a case because the government does not care for foreign behavior. The BTIR noted that one of the keys to bringing a case in Thailand is a complaint from a Thai firm. The FTI and the Joint WTO Committee indicated that Thai firms rarely consider filing such complaints because few United States imports compete with domestically made Thai goods. Moreover, the industry representatives all stated that when American products do compete with Thai goods, Thai firms still hesitate to file a complaint because most Thai firms that find themselves competing with United States goods also have extensive import operations. These firms therefore have conflicting interests, for while their local production operations might incline them toward filing a complaint alleging American dumping and/or subsidies, their import activities push them in the opposite direction since any restrictions on trade due to Thai AD or CVD duties would hurt their import line of business.

An interesting illustration of how conflicting Thai business interests confound Thai retaliation was found in the 2005 interviews, where the Bureau of Multilateral Trade Negotiations (BMTN) respondents noted that Thailand has chosen not to sanction the United States over the Byrd Amendment (see chapter 2). As the reader may recall, several countries, including Thailand, won a WTO case that had challenged the Byrd Amendment. These countries were authorized to penalize American goods entering their markets. While several WTO members have imposed sanctions, the BMTN stated that Thailand has decided to wait to do so. This decision was attributed to the possible harm that restricting American products might do to Thai importers. The Thais hope that in the meantime the Byrd Amendment will be rescinded, thus eliminating the need for retaliation.

Regarding Thai government retaliation at the WTO and elsewhere by taking positions that oppose the United States, the BTIR officials said that Thailand does not engage in such behavior. Apparently, there was a concern that engaging in such actions would be counterproductive, especially if the United States came to believe that retaliation motivated the Thai negotiating position. Instead, the BTIR argued that Thailand only opposed American positions when it felt that the United States was in error. The United States position on worker's rights during the Seattle and Doha WTO conferences was offered as an example. At those meetings, Thai representatives felt that the American demands for some sort of international code to set employment standards would work to the detriment of Thailand, given the Thai advantage as far as low cost labor is concerned. Hence, the Thai representatives opposed the American position.

Turning to the issue of appeals, Thai government officials from the BTIR and from the BMTN and industry representatives from the Thai Iron and Steel Industry Club (TISIC), the Thai Food Processors' Association (TFPA), and the Thai Pineapple Packers' Group (TPPG) stated that for the most part, private industry conducts its appeals of AD decisions in the United States court system, while the government takes its CVD cases to the WTO. On occasion, however, the government utilizes United States courts for CVD appeals. Beginning with industry experiences in American courts, the TISIC, the TFPA, and the TPPG respondents all mentioned that businesses from their organizations had filed appeals to the United States Court of International Trade. In each case, the appeal focused on contesting the procedures the Department of Commerce (DOC) used when calculating dumping rates. The Thai plaintiffs won each time, but in a pineapple case the United States Court of Appeals for the Federal Circuit partially overturned the lower court ruling. In the pineapple case, the Appeals Court upheld the lower court as far as its reversal of DOC cost of production calculations were concerned, but reversed the lower court over the question of the time period for which duties could be assessed.[21]

As far as their beliefs about the fairness of the United States appeals system were concerned, each of the industry group respondents stated that they had confidence in the American process. This was not surprising, given the experiences the members of these groups have had when utilizing the system in the United States. The TPPG representative did note, however, that the United States appeals process was extremely time consuming and expensive. These time commitments and expenses were regarded as putting some Thai firms at a disadvantage when they attempted to obtain redress for such grievances as they might have regarding the American unfair trade process.

In the 2005 interviews, officials from the BTIR stated that some Thai firms have started employing Washington lobbyists as a means for pressuring the Department of Commerce to reconsider its actions during AD investigations. The use of lobbyists was described as a supplement to the appeals process. According to the BTIR interviewees, this use of lobbyists has thus far had no effect on the DOC, in part because of the way American law structures AD investigations and in part because the DOC tends to be more responsive to American complainants than to foreign firms.

With respect to the WTO appeal system, the BTIR and the BMTN officials argued that while the WTO provided a useful vehicle for challenging the actions of other countries, it has several problems. One is the long period of time involved in WTO appeals, which sometimes consume several years before final resolutions are reached. Another is the expense associated with WTO cases, which can cost far more than the Thai government can afford to spend. A third involves the human costs of properly training Thai personnel and assigning them to spend large amounts of time on WTO appeals. And finally, the Thais mentioned the problem of enforcement, pointing out that it is difficult to force such large countries as the United States to abide by adverse WTO rulings. As a result, the BTIR and the BMTN respondents all stated that the Thais prefer to engage in WTO cases only if they can act together with several countries. The BMTN official offered as an example the recent challenge in the WTO to the American law that channels unfair trade duties to private American firms instead of to the United States treasury (the Byrd Amendment, see chapter 2). In the Byrd Amendment case before the WTO, Thailand joined eight other countries in arguing that the United States law violated WTO rules. By working with other countries, the Thais feel that not only is their chance of success greater, but that the United States is more likely to respect an adverse WTO ruling since a failure to do so might lead to retaliatory trade restrictions from several countries and not just from Thailand.

Negotiations

This collection of questions examined the respondents' attitudes toward current WTO AD and CVD rules, the degree to which Thailand participated in the Uruguay Round negotiations that established the present rules, and how the Thais plan to conduct themselves in future negotiations regarding unfair trade rules. The government officials answering these questions were from the Bureau of Trade Interests and Remedies (BTIR), the Bureau of Multilateral Trade Negotiations (BMTN), the Board of Investment (BOI), and the Bank of Thailand (BOT). The private industry respondents included representatives from the Thai Iron and Steel Industry Club (TISIC), the Federation of Thai Industries (FTI), and the Joint WTO Committee.

The first question dealt with how the Thais feel about the current WTO AD and CVD rules. Every respondent from industry and from the government answered that the WTO rules now in existence were unfair because they benefit large and advanced countries and penalize developing countries. The BTIR officials noted that this was largely due to the fact that current WTO rules are patterned on drafts submitted by such large countries as the United States, the European Union, and Canada. These officials and their colleagues from the BMTN maintained that patterning WTO rules on the large country drafts meant that the rules would work to the advantage of advanced countries and would hurt the ability of smaller countries to engage in the export activities needed to promote economic growth and development.

Another issue pertaining to current rules has to do with their complexity. Officials from the BMTN and from the BOI argued that WTO rules are so arcane that countries must have large staffs of highly trained experts in order to understand the rules and the many nuances they contain. These respondents stated that since few developing countries have such experts, they are at a severe disadvantage when compared to advanced societies that do have such trained personnel. In addition, the BMTN interviewees maintained that WTO regulations have so many loopholes that they do not constrain countries wishing to use AD and CVD actions as protectionist devices.

When asked about the role Thailand played during the Uruguay Round negotiations that established the current rules, the official from the BMTN stated that Thailand had little influence because it lacked both the experience with AD and CVD laws and the staff of experts needed to participate actively. The interviewees from the FTI and the Joint WTO Committee concurred with this view about the lack of expertise during the Uruguay Round and noted that one of Thailand's most important trade-related problems was to develop the needed expertise so that the country could participate more effectively in WTO negotiations.

The remaining questions in this section related to Thai plans for future WTO negotiations. All respondents, both governmental and private, maintained that Thailand needs to take a "get tough" approach toward future discussions. As mentioned above, all respondents regard trade as a vital Thai national interest and see foreign AD and CVD actions as severely hurting Thailand. Every interviewee also felt that the WTO negotiating process was an important arena for obtaining changes in foreign AD and CVD rules. Thus, the respondents all argued in favor of a more vigorous Thai position in the future. Among private sector respondents, the TISIC representative was especially interested in using WTO negotiations to secure changes in AD and CVD rules. Given the history of the Thai steel industry as far as AD and CVD investigations are concerned, the TISIC position was as expected.

Finally, the BTIR and the BMTN officials stated that Thailand plans to cooperate with other countries to change AD and CVD rules in future WTO negotiations. These officials noted that Thai representatives have already engaged in such cooperative efforts with EU and Japanese negotiators during the Doha Conference in November 2001. They also suggested that a closer working relationship with the Association of Southeast Asian Nations (ASEAN) is under consideration. In addition, the BMTN representative pointed out that in 2003 and early 2004 Thailand joined with several countries (Brazil, Chile, Colombia, Costa Rica, China, Israel, Japan, Korea, Mexico, Norway, Taiwan, Singapore, Switzerland, and Turkey) to form a "Friends of Antidumping" group to push for changes in the WTO's AD rules. Of special interest to the BMTN were tighter regulations on the use of the best information available during AD investigations, revisions in the procedures for calculating AD duties, and new "sunset" rules that would automatically terminate AD duties after five years. Beyond this, a BOI official explained that Thailand sought alterations in CVD regulations that would revise cumulation rules and alter the traffic light approach to subsidies (see chapter 2 for explanations of these terms). The respondent from the Joint WTO Committee also expressed an interest in having the de minimis levels for AD actions increased from 2 percent to 5 percent and agreed that there is a need to restrict the occasions on which the best information available may be used.

The industry respondents from the FTI and the Joint WTO Committee added that many of the larger companies in the Thai private sector are working to set up ties with their counterparts in other countries in an effort to increase the pressures on governments to push for AD and CVD rules changes at the WTO. These respondents noted that initial efforts to establish such ties began at the Seattle WTO conference in November 1999 and that more energy would be devoted to the project in the future. For the reasons noted above, the FTI and the Joint WTO Committee interviewees pointed out that the steel industry has been particularly active in this area.

The TISIC respondents noted in the 2005 interviews that they have been actively pushing for another type of negotiations regarding unfair trade rules. These pertain to the creation of a free trade agreement (FTA) between Thailand and the United States. The TISIC spokespersons expressed the belief that an FTA might lead to modifications in the way United States unfair trade rules would apply to Thai producers. Apparently, the TISIC interviewees believed that Canada and Mexico are receiving special antidumping treatment as a result of membership in the North American Free Trade Agreement (NAFTA) and were hopeful that an FTA between the United States and Thailand would lead to a similar arrangement for Thai producers.[22] While discussions pertaining to a possible FTA have been held, there have been no indications to date that American negotiations are prepared to accept special unfair trade provisions for Thailand.

Another avenue for seeking a relaxation of American unfair trade rules was described by a BTIR respondent in 2005. This involved an effort by the Thai Ministry of Commerce (MOC) to use American concerns over terrorism as leverage to push for a better deal regarding unfair trade. The official observed that Thailand has a substantial Islamic minority population, some of whom might be inclined toward extremist activity if United States trade restrictions affected their prospects for employment or if such restrictions were perceived as an American attempt to dominate a non-Western society.[23] As of early 2005, however, American negotiators had not been willing to accept the Ministry of Commerce contention that there is a linkage between unfair trade regulations and the incidence of terrorism.

A final tactic the BTIR noted that Thai companies were employing as a complement to negotiations involves lobbying members of Congress to relax selected American unfair trade regulations. Additionally, these lobbying efforts have been aimed at creating an atmosphere in Congress that would be receptive to any alterations or compromises that might emerge from ongoing WTO talks regarding AD and CVD rules and procedures. To date, the Thais believe that this lobbying has brought only modest success.

Impact Issues

This group of questions pertained to the political and economic effects on Thailand of United States AD and CVD actions. The issues covered included whether restrictions due to unfair trade create worker unrest due to unemployment and problems in maintaining Thai economic growth and development. In addition, the interviewees were asked if American AD and CVD actions force Thai firms into bankruptcy and whether the Thai government provides assistance to Thai firms that are adversely affected by United States AD and CVD investigations. The only respondents to these questions came from the Bureau of Trade Interests and Remedies (BTIR), the Thai Food Processors' Association (TFPA), and the Thai Iron and Steel Industry Club (TISIC).

Starting with the questions about worker unrest, the maintenance of economic growth, and bankruptcy, each respondent stated that unrest and bankruptcy have not yet been problems. The BTIR official noted that American AD and CVD actions have hurt Thai companies because these actions have resulted in lost sales, but the TFPA representative maintained that unduly adverse consequences have been avoided up to this point because the affected Thai companies have searched diligently for new markets. As for the question of growth, the TISIC interviewee pointed out that since the United States is Thailand's largest export market, anything, such as AD and CVD measures, that even partially closes that market would naturally have negative consequences for the ability to promote economic growth. It was explained in the 2005 follow-up, however, that international market conditions can lessen the effect of a reduced access to the American market.

Whereas in 2000 a limited access to the United States had a serious effect on Thai steel producers, by 2005 the surging demand for steel in China offered an alternative market that the Thais have been quick to exploit. Given the rapidly expanding volume of steel production in China, such alternative opportunities were not expected to last over the long run. Therefore, American market restrictions were still a source of serious concern.

With regard to the question of government assistance to firms affected by AD and CVD actions, the BTIR official commented that the Thai Ministry of Commerce (MOC) tries to do all it can to help firms locate new markets to replace any that are lost in the United States. It was noted, however, that the assistance is very general and primarily consists of advice about what foreign markets might be available. For the most part, it was explained that private firms were expected to do the bulk of the work associated with finding markets. The industry representatives from the TFPA and the TISIC both indicated that despite the government's best efforts, the primary burden for locating new and replacement markets fell on the shoulders of private corporations and that the task is extremely daunting, given the highly competitive nature of international commerce. Thus, all interviewees agreed that while American AD and CVD actions have not yet produced either social instability or slower economic growth, the impact of those actions has meant lost business and the constant need to seek out new and/or replacement markets. Fortunately, the economic boom in China has offered at least a short-term answer to the need for new business opportunities.

Chapter Summary

This chapter examined four subjects: (1) the Thai position in the world economy and as a trading partner with the United States, (2) the types of AD and CVD cases that have been brought against Thai exporters by the United States, (3) the Thai government agencies that handle trade policy and the key Thai business groups in the iron and steel and canned pineapple industries, and (4) the results from a survey that was conducted among Thai government trade agencies and business groups representing the iron and steel and canned pineapple industries.

An examination of World Trade Organization (WTO) and United States trading data revealed that since 1995 Thailand has ranked as one of the world's twenty-five largest importers and exporters. Only seven developing countries rank ahead of Thailand in this regard. It also was found that Thailand produces approximately one percent of world exports and consumes about the same quantity of international imports.

When the United States–Thai trade picture was considered, it was determined that the relationship is asymmetrical, with the United States playing the dominant role. From the Thai point of view, since 1995 the United States has served as Thailand's largest export market and as its second largest source of imports. For the United States, Thailand is one of the top fifteen sources of imports and among the twenty-six largest markets for United States exports. Only nine developing countries have more trade with the United States than does Thailand.

Thailand also figures prominently as a target of American AD and CVD complaints. Since the United States first imposed AD and CVD duties on Thai goods in 1985, Thailand has ranked as the ninth most frequent developing country target for American AD and CVD investigations. The primary Thai industry that has been hit by AD and CVD investigations has been iron and steel producers, which have been the subject of 62 percent of all Thai AD filings and 70 percent of all CVD complaints. In this regard, Thai complaints reflect the typical pattern found among all American AD and CVD cases, which tend to focus on the iron and steel industry.

Due to the prominence of the iron and steel industry as far as AD and CVD cases are concerned, the survey of Thai government trading agencies and private industry groups focused on the problems faced by iron and steel producers. The canned pineapple industry also was examined to provide an agricultural basis for comparison. The survey was designed to uncover the problems and complaints Thai government officials and industry representatives have as far as American AD and CVD cases are concerned. As was described earlier, these interviews focused on nine categories of questions relating to how respondents view United States AD and CVD procedures, the degree to which they attempt to challenge American AD and CVD findings before United States courts and/or within the WTO dispute settlement system, and whether they support attempts to negotiate new WTO rules to limit the AD and CVD practices of member countries.

Based upon these interviews, it is possible to make several observations about the Thai experience with United States AD and CVD practices. The first is that despite the fact that the Thais consider trade a vital national interest, both the governmental and private industry respondents felt that there is a deficiency in Thailand of experts with the training and knowledge to understand both United States and WTO rules and procedures with regard to AD and CVD cases. In addition, it was uniformly noted that the primary source available to provide training for the Thais was the American attorneys hired to assist with the AD and CVD cases the Thais faced. This lack of expertise clearly leaves the Thais at a disadvantage both with regard to the

individual AD and CVD cases they confront and during international negotiations to modify WTO AD and CVD rules. While the government has initiated recent efforts to provide educational assistance to Thai companies, it
was generally believed that these efforts have thus far been ineffective because they have not provided sufficient details about American and WTO
rules, procedures, and decision-making processes.

Having said this, it should be pointed out that most of the Thai officials
interviewed displayed a relatively sophisticated understanding of United
States and WTO AD and CVD rules and procedures. After all, there was a
widespread understanding of the role the best information available could
play in American investigations and of the opportunity for appeals in the
United States and at the WTO. Moreover, when discussing their goals for future multilateral talks during the Doha Round, Thai respondents were very
familiar with the methods used to calculate AD and CVD duties, the problems associated with sunset reviews, the use of cumulation and de minimis
rules, the traffic light approach to subsidies, and many other aspects of American and WTO rules. Hence, although it may be fair to conclude that the
Thais have shortcomings regarding sufficient numbers of trained specialists
and regarding some of the more arcane aspects of international regulations,
it would be inaccurate to conclude that Thailand is bereft of the means for
handling many of the unfair trade problems it confronts. Still, the heavy reliance on American trade lawyers for training Thai specialists is something
that should be remedied.

A second observation relates to the Thai feeling that American AD and
CVD investigations are frequently initiated to harass Thai companies and
are conducted without a proper respect for Thai sovereignty. The possible use
of the best information available was regarded as a pressure tactic for forcing
the Thais to conform to American demands, and the complexity and expenses associated with investigations were seen as so excessive that smaller
Thai companies sometimes were hard-pressed to cope with those costs and
were often forced to consider abandoning the American market.

A third observation has to do with how the Thais react to United States
investigations. First, the Thais do not attempt to retaliate. For one thing,
there are obstacles in Thai law that prevent the imposition of AD and CVD
duties on a retaliatory basis. Retaliation during WTO and other international negotiations also has been foresworn due to the belief that it would be
counterproductive. Second, the Thais rarely try to reach settlements to suspend American investigations. Instead, there is a preference for seeing cases
through to their conclusion and using the United States court system to
challenge adverse rulings. Additionally, some Thai firms are attempting to

use the open nature of the American political system to their advantage by hiring attorneys to monitor United States AD complaints and by working with lobbyists to try to bring political influence to bear on the Commerce Department officials who handle AD cases. Finally, Thai companies have worked hard to find alternative markets to replace the business they have lost in the United States due to adverse AD and CVD decisions. The recent economic boom in China has been valuable in this regard. Presumably, rapid growth in other parts of the developing world also would provide useful export opportunities.

A fourth observation pertains to Thai intentions regarding future WTO negotiations over AD and CVD rules. As might be expected, the Thais are strongly interested in modifying WTO rules in such a way as to restrict their use by larger countries. At the same time, the Thais feel that their relatively small size and lack of expertise relative to the United States and other prominent WTO members leaves them at a severe disadvantage. To compensate for these problems, the Thai government is pursuing a strategy that calls for forming coalitions with other countries that share Thai concerns. The Friends of Antidumping is an example of such an alliance. In addition, Thai corporations are seeking closer relations with private firms in other societies in an effort to put as much pressure as possible on governments to alter WTO AD and CVD regulations.

A final observation is that Thailand is seeking to use international political and economic conditions and the American international agenda to its advantage. One instance of this is found in the attempt to exploit the United States interest in free trade agreements with some developing countries to secure favorable treatment as regards unfair trade.[24] Another example is the effort to link the war on terrorism to a relaxation of unfair trade regulations. In both cases, the Thai government has played on opportunities as they have presented themselves to try to gain an advantage for itself in its largest export market. Thus far, neither effort has paid off as the Thais wished, but one can presume that the Thais will continue to try to tie trade to larger political and strategic issues both in bilateral relations and in multilateral trade negotiations at the WTO.

To conclude, United States AD and CVD rules and procedures obviously pose serious problems for Thailand. In part, these problems pertain to the lack of Thai expertise and to the way in which the United States conducts its investigations. Beyond this, the immense costs of unfair trade investigations lead to severe difficulties, as do the complications associated with conducting WTO negotiations. Clearly, the Thai national interest would be served by establishing better training programs in Thai universities and on the part of the Thai government and by pursuing a vigorous WTO campaign to secure new international AD and CVD standards. More specific suggestions regarding these matters are included in the next chapter.

Notes

1. U.S. Department of Commerce, International Trade Administration, *U.S. Foreign Trade Highlights*, Washington, DC: U.S. Department of Commerce, 2002.

2. U.S. Department of Commerce, International Trade Administration, *U.S. Foreign Trade Highlights-Trade and Economy: Data and Analysis*, October 31, 2001, available from www.ita.doc.gov/td/industry/otea/usfth/aggregate/hl00t10; and U.S. Department of Commerce, International Trade Administration, *U.S. Foreign Trade Highlights-Trade and Economy: Data and Analysis*, October 31, 2002, available from www.ita.doc.gov/td/industry/otea/usfth/aggregate/hl00t11.html.

3. James Caporaso, "Dependence, Dependency, and Power in the Global System," *International Organization*, vol. 32, no. 1, Winter 1978, pp. 13–44.

4. U.S. Department of Commerce, International Trade Administration, *Sunset Review Update*, 1999, available from http://web.ita.gov/ia/suncase.nsf/; and U.S. Department of Commerce, International Trade Administration, *Sunset Review: Textile and Textile Products from Thailand*, 2000, available from http://web.ita.doc.gov/ia/suncase.nsf/.

5. U.S. Department of Commerce, International Trade Administration, *AD and CVD Investigation Decisions*, 2000 and 2001, available from http://ia.ita.doc/states/caselist.txt.

6. Howard P. Marvel and Edward John Ray, "Countervailing Duties," *The Economic Journal*, vol. 105, November 1995, pp. 1576–93; I. M. Destler, *American Trade Politics*, Washington, DC: Institute for International Economics, 1995, pp. 157–59; World Trade Organization, *International Trade Statistics*, Geneva, 2001; World Trade Organization, CV Measures: By Sector, available from www.wto.org; World Trade Organization, AD Initiations: By Sector, available from www.wto.org.

7. Thai Bureau of Trade Interests and Remedies, Department of Foreign Trade, Ministry of Commerce, *A Guide to the Bureau of Trade Interests and Remedies* [Brochure], translated by Benjamas Chinapandhu, Nonthaburi, Thailand: Bureau of Trade Interests and Remedies, 2002.

8. Thai Bureau of Multilateral Trade Negotiations, Department of Business Economics, Thai Ministry of Commerce, *A History of the Department of Business Economics* [Brochure], translated by Benjamas Chinapandhu, Bangkok: Bureau of Multilateral Trade Negotiations, 2002.

9. Office of the Board of Investment, Office of the Prime Minister, Royal Thai Government, *A Guide to the Board of Investment* [Brochure], Bangkok: The Office of the Board of Investment, 2000.

10. Credit and Refinancing Division, Financial Markets and Operations Group, Bank of Thailand, *Summary of the Bank of Thailand's Financial Assistance to Priority Economic Sectors* [Brochure], Bangkok: The Bank of Thailand, August 14, 2001.

11. Joint WTO Committee (Thailand), *WTO Thailand*, 2001, translated by Benjamas Chinapandhu, available from www.fti.or.th/nfti/org/index-e.html.

12. Federation of Thai Industries, *Organization and Industry Clubs*, 2001, available from www.fti.or.th/nfti/org/index-e.html.

13. Federation of Thai Industries, *Industry Chapter: Raw Material Products-Iron and Steel*, 2001, available from www.fti.or.th/club115.htm.

14. Thai Food Processors' Association, *The Regulations of the Thai Food Processors' Association*, August 24, 2001, translated by Benjamas Chinapandhu, Bangkok: The Thai Food Processors' Association, available from www.thaifood.org/rule/rule2.htm.

15. Food Market Exchange, *The Pineapple Market: A Review of the News in 2001*, January 16, 2002, available from www.foodmarketexchange.com/datacenter/industry/article/idf-pineapple-.

16. This research has been approved by the Institutional Review Board for Human Subjects Research at Miami University in Oxford, Ohio.

17. Bureau of Trade Interest and Remedies, Department of Foreign Trade, Thai Ministry of Commerce, *Thai Products Imposed by Antidumping and Countervailing Duty Measures from Trading Partners* [Brochure], translated by Benjamas Chinapandhu, Nonthaburi, Thailand: Bureau of Trade Interests and Remedies, April 2002.

18. The reader is reminded that dumping is when the price in the United States is lower than a comparison price obtained either by looking at the price in the home market, in another export market, or by constructing a comparison price. When such a comparison indicates that the foreign price is lower, then one has a negative margin, which is the opposite of dumping.

19. In the 2005 follow-up interview, the BTIR respondents noted that American questionnaires are now available on the Internet, which assists somewhat in meeting the timetable for submitting the responses during an investigation. There were still complaints, however, that the deadlines for completing the questionnaires were unreasonable.

20. Arkon Situbtim, "Analysis and Evaluation: The Impact of Antidumping on Thai Canned Pineapple in the U.S. market," Thai Bureau of Trade Interests and Remedies, Department of Foreign Trade, Ministry of Commerce Working Paper, March 2002.

21. United States Court of Appeals for the Federal Circuit, *Thai Pineapple Canning Industry Corp. and Mitsubishi International Corp. v. United States and Maui Pineapple Co., Ltd and International Longshoremen's and Warehousemen's Union*, decided December 6, 2001.

22. The only special treatment regarding AD and CVD rules accorded under NAFTA relates to a provision specifying that more restrictive American unfair trade rules only will apply if Congress states that the rules are meant to apply to NAFTA partners. See John M. Rothgeb, Jr., *U.S. Trade Policy: Balancing Economic Dreams and Political Realities*, Washington, DC: CQ Press, 2001, p. 202; Steve Dryden, *Trade Warriors: USTR and the American Crusade for Free Trade*, New York: Oxford University Press, 1995, p. 342; Raymond Vernon, Debora L. Spar, and Glenn Tobin, *Iron Trian-*

gles and Revolving Doors: Cases in U.S. Foreign Economic Policymaking, New York: Praeger Publishers, 1991, p. 47.

23. It should be noted that Moslems constitute approximately 5 percent of the total Thai population. Most Moslems live in the four southern provinces of Narathiwas, Pattanee, Satun, and Yala. In the these provinces, Moslems constitute between 70 and 82 percent of the population. This part of Thailand, which is located near the border with Malaysia, has been the scene of some religiously based unrest. See National Statistical Office of Thailand, "Summary of the Survey from Cultural Activities Participation in the Year 2005," Bangkok, 2006, Thai Southern Border Provinces Administration Center, "Percentage of Islamics in 4 Southern Provinces," Yala, 2006, and U.S. Department of State, Bureau of East Asian and Pacific Affairs, "Background Note: Thailand," October 2005, available at www.state.gov.

24. For a discussion of the United States interest in free trade agreements, see Neil King, Jr., "U.S. to Expand Trade Pacts," *Wall Street Journal,* October 25, 2002, p. A4 and Simon Romero, "Frustrated, U.S. Will Seek Bilateral Trade Pacts," *New York Times,* November 19, 2003, p. C2.

CHAPTER FOUR

~

Conclusions and Implications

Having completed the examination of the evolution of American antidumping and countervailing duty regulations and of the Thai reactions to those rules and procedures, attention now turns to the implications of this research for policy making in Thailand and other developing countries and to the conclusions that can be drawn from the foregoing analysis. This chapter will focus first on the question of policy recommendations and then will consider what the findings herein say about international development.

Policy Recommendations

The policy recommendations that can be derived from this research take four forms. The first relates to the domestic changes that can be made in Thailand. The second has to do with how the WTO can more effectively serve the interests of developing countries. The third pertains to how the Thais and other developing countries can best represent their interests in the United States. Finally, there is the question of the course Thailand and other developing societies should take in international trade negotiations.

Domestic Reforms in Thailand

The recommendations regarding domestic reforms primarily relate to educational and information efforts. As the reader may recall, one of the most persistently heard complaints to emerge from the interviews with Thai government officials and private industry representatives related to the limited number of Thai experts with training in American and international trade law and policy and to the problems that were encountered when attempting to obtain the necessary information about unfair trade investigation rules and procedures. Given the statements that one respondent after another made regarding the preeminent position trade holds as a Thai national interest, it was surprising to see that both in the initial interviews and in the 2005 follow-ups that the dearth of Thai trade specialists and the paucity of information stood out as a major problems. Clearly, action should be taken to address this situation.

One important move that the Thais should take to create a larger body of experts would be to expand programs at Thai universities that can provide interested students and officials with the preparation they need to advise the government and private corporations regarding the trade laws and procedures found in the United States, the European Union, the WTO, and other major international commercial actors and markets. It might even be advisable to require that Thai law schools include in their curriculum courses relating to foreign trade. Private firms and industry groups should take an active role in creating these programs by interacting with university scholars and administrators to ensure that they meet the needs of those who engage in international trade. Once these programs are established, it might be advisable to create incentives to encourage corporate executives and governmental officials to participate in these educational opportunities. At least initially, it may be necessary for the staffing for these programs to come from foreign experts, including academics from the United States and other countries, WTO officials, and foreign attorneys specializing in international trade. As time passes and a group of Thai experts develops, staffing can be passed to local specialists.

Another educational effort for the Thais to consider would be the establishment of scholarship opportunities to encourage Thai students to study trade policy and trade law at colleges and universities in the United States, in the European Union, and in other societies where such educational opportunities are available. These scholarships might be created both by the government and by private firms and industry groups. Additionally, the Thais might set up a program to send government officials and industry representatives to the many intensive week-long and month-long executive-level trade seminars that are offered by some American colleges and universities. Establishing programs of these types would allow Thailand to begin closing the knowledge gap that currently hampers its responses to AD and CVD cases. A larger pool of local experts also would reduce the Thai dependence on the foreign trade lawyers and experts who currently look after Thai interests. Moreover, more domestic experts would enhance the Thai ability to play a more active role at the WTO and during international negotiations.

Another recommendation that should complement the just mentioned educational efforts would be for the Thai government to put a major effort into locating and cataloging the many information sources available on the Internet that pertain to American trade policy and to the WTO. As can be seen from even a cursory examination of the websites maintained by such United States government agencies as the Office of the United States Trade Representative, the International Trade Commission, and the International Trade Administration, a large portion of the information needed to understand the procedures associated with AD and CVD investigations in the United States is available on the Internet. The same is true for matters relating to unfair cases in the European Union and in other countries and for the WTO. The Thai government would be providing a valuable service to Thai producers if it assembled this information, translated at least part of it, and made it available to interested parties in Thailand. In addition, instruction should be offered regarding the procedures for locating the proper information at websites.

The World Trade Organization
There are several things the WTO can do to help developing countries as they grapple with unfair trade. Most of the recommendations for the WTO relate to education, training, and information, but the WTO might also play a role as an intermediary during AD and CVD investigations. At the outset, it should be recognized that as an international organization with over 150 members, both advanced and developing, the WTO must maintain its status as a neutral party. Even within the confines of neutrality, however, the WTO can take important steps to assist its developing members.

Beginning with education, training, and information, the WTO can take action in several areas. The first would involve expanding the training seminars that the WTO currently conducts for developing countries. As the Thais noted in the 2005 interviews, while the WTO seminars that were held early on were not particularly useful, by 2002 these sessions had been reorganized and were providing the type of assistance that Thai respondents felt they needed. The WTO should continue such efforts and should work closely with government officials and industry representatives in developing countries to determine the types of assistance they most need.

Another educational move would call for the WTO to consult with universities in the developing world to help set up the appropriate educational programs regarding trade. In giving this assistance, the WTO might provide support staff and instructors on a temporary basis and might help locate scholars and specialists from advanced countries who could act as instructors while these programs were in their developmental phases. In addition, the WTO should consider maintaining a reference service to help developing countries locate foreign academic institutions for students who need to study abroad.

A second recommendation is that the WTO set up a reference service pertaining to unfair trade rules and procedures in the United States, the European Union, and other countries where AD and CVD cases are most frequently filed. As was noted above when discussing the need for the Thai government to put together a service of this sort, a data bank could save developing country actors considerable trouble when they confront unfair trade cases. In a related move, the WTO could provide technical experts to act as consultants to developing (and other) actors during AD and CVD investigations.

The WTO also could help those confronting unfair trade investigations if it had information of another type: the names of attorneys who handle unfair trade cases and a system for rating the experience and specialties of those attorneys. One of the most important of the findings to emerge from the interviews reported in chapter 3 had to do with the degree to which the Thais rely on foreign attorneys during AD and CVD investigations. In addition, it was found that Thai firms often had problems locating attorneys and that on occasion the attorneys they hired did not perform as expected. No doubt, other developing countries are in the same position and confront similar obstacles. Given this dependence, which was mentioned both in 2000 and in the 2005 follow-up and is not likely to change soon, the WTO would be providing a valuable service if it made available information about the lawyers who handle AD and CVD cases in the United States and elsewhere.

A final step the WTO might consider involves serving as an intermediary during AD and CVD investigations. As Thai business representatives and government officials stated, questions frequently arise during investigations regarding whether foreigners are requesting appropriate information. Private industry respondents maintained that American investigators sometimes asked for data that might give competitors an edge and government officials argued that on occasion the information requested involved confidential tax records. In both cases, the Thai interviewees claimed that they confronted a dilemma, for they either could protect an important area of secrecy and face the use of the best information available, or they could avoid BIA, but lose secrecy. These are the circumstances where a WTO mediator might be used to seek a resolution that provided the proper data while limiting the revelation of proprietary information.

Thai Interests in the United States

In the 2005 follow-up interviews, Thai respondents stated that Thai corporations have begun to employ American lobbyists to seek more favorable treatment from the United States Department of Commerce (DOC) and to convince members of Congress to accept alterations in American unfair trade laws. There also has been a recent effort to tie a relaxation of AD and CVD regulations to the American war on terrorism. The Thai lobbying efforts with the DOC no doubt reflects domestic practice in Thailand, where corporations seeking political influence often work through industry groups and/or current and former bureaucrats to affect the way government agencies handle their cases. As a considerable body of research shows, such lobbying with administrative agencies is far less effective in the United States, particularly when one is dealing with AD and CVD cases.[1] One reason for this is that American AD and CVD laws have been structured by Congress to leave as little discretion as possible to the administrative agencies that handle those laws.[2] Moreover, as the discussion in chapter 2 indicated, Congress has made it clear that it expects the DOC to act vigorously to protect the interests first and foremost of American firms when handling unfair trade. This was the purpose Congress was attempting to serve when it transferred administrative control over AD and CVD investigations from the Treasury Department to the Commerce Department in 1979. Hence, lobbying activity directed toward the DOC is likely to yield far less than the Thais might wish.

More effective lobbying is directed at members of Congress and at the White House. In addition, one needs to make arguments that relate to important American interests and to forge domestic and foreign alliances to reinforce one's claims and to finance the lobbying activity. This is where the assertions about terrorism might play a role, for past presidents and Congresses have demonstrated a willingness to respond favorably to arguments that tied trade to broader American foreign policy and national security goals. For example, as the fascist threat mounted in the 1930s and early 1940s, Congress whittled away at the neutrality acts that forbid certain types of American trade with belligerents. During the Cold War, presidents from Truman through Reagan pushed continually and successfully for relaxations by Congress of a variety of American trade restrictions to help in the struggle against communism.[3] Indeed, it was in part White House pressures to lower barriers to fairly traded goods during the Cold War that prompted Congress to extend the scope of unfair trade regulations, as was described in chapter 2.

These previous experiences suggest that the president and Congress sometimes respond when there is a convincing link between trade and national security. The war on terror may give the Thais a chance to make such a connection. In making their case, the Thais must do several things. First and foremost, the arguments made must be specific and backed by credible evidence. Simply asserting that the vigorous application of AD and/or CVD rules will affect terrorism or sympathy for terrorists in Thailand or Southeast Asia will not do. Instead, the Thais must show that commercial limitations due to unfair trade restrictions lead to resentment and breeds support for anti-American or anti-Western groups who finance and support terrorist acts. In the absence of such evidence, it is unlikely that the trade-terrorist link will get much attention in Washington.

The second thing the Thais must do is to focus their efforts on the White House and on carefully identified members of Congress. Concentrating on the White House is essential because most Americans and many in Congress take their national security cues from the president. If the president and/or his closest advisers are convinced of a connection between trade and terror, and more specifically between the application of unfair trade regulations and support for terrorists, then many in Congress will accept the idea. Of course, this will not guarantee Congressional action to loosen unfair trade rules, but it may enhance the prospects for such action, particularly if the ongoing international trade negotiations associated with the Doha Round produces a package deal that ties action on unfair trade to concessions the United States seeks in other areas.

Third, it is important that the Thais seek out other developing countries to act as partners in making the trade-terror case. If actors from several countries make the argument, it will appear more credible. The same can be said of such supporting evidence as is available, for evidence from several sources is more convincing than if it comes from a single actor. Working with other countries also would spread the expenses associated with lobbying and would buttress any other arguments that might be made regarding limiting unfair trade regulations. Indeed, it might prove useful for the Thais to cooperate with other countries in lobbying Congress to change such things as sunset review regulations, the use of the best information available, de minimis limits, and other technical matters that currently are a source of irritation for Thai traders.

Finally, the Thai lobbying effort should seek to act in concert with American corporations that either do business in Thailand or that consume goods made in Thailand. Both types of firms have a vested interest in an unfettered Thai access to the United States market. Support from these companies could provide a valuable boost to the Thai attempt to push for a favorable hearing in Congress, especially if the firms in question have operations in a member's district. One thing American-based firms can do is demonstrate that inputs from their operations or from their partners in Thailand and other developing countries allow for more efficient production that allows for continued operations by the units that they have in the United States. Members of Congress often are responsive to such assertions because it touches on the question of jobs for their constituents.

As the Thais move ahead with lobbying, it should be understood that Congress traditionally takes a tough view of unfair trade legislation, as was illustrated in chapter 2. Therefore, lobbying efforts, whether related to the association between trade and terror or to other issues, must be part of a larger package that not only links trade to broader foreign policy and national security goals, but that also is associated with international negotiations at the WTO.

International Trade Negotiations
One result to emerge from the interviews in Thailand is that the Thais have a firm grasp both of the AD and CVD issues they wish to pursue in WTO negotiations and of the need to form partnerships with other countries as they bargain. Starting with partnerships, the Thai participation in the Friends of Antidumping group is just the sort of alliance that should increase the probability of success during WTO talks about AD and CVD rules and procedures. As the Thais recognize, individual developing country voices are not nearly as strong as they become when collected into a coalition. As noted above, one recommendation for enhancing the value of the Friends of Antidumping is that it expand its activities to include domestic lobbying in the United States, the European Union, and elsewhere.

As far as issues for WTO talks are concerned, the Thais have identified five areas to concentrate on during negotiations: (1) changes in de minimis rules, (2) alterations in the use of cumulation, (3) modifying constructed value regulations, (4) revisions in the use of the best information available, and (5) adjusting sunset review procedures. Beginning with de minimis rules, it should be clear from the discussion in chapters two and three that under current WTO regulations, the Thais believe that de minimis levels are so low that they invite corporations in the United States and other countries to use AD and CVD cases to harass competitors from the developing world. As the Thais see it, a low de minimis greatly increases the probability that the DOC will find that dumping or subsidies exist. This in turn means that American firms have a good prospect of success if they file complaints, thus encouraging them to do so. Raising the de minimis might reduce such behavior by making positive dumping or subsidy findings less likely.

Revising the WTO's cumulation rules also might reduce the likelihood that unfair trade rules would be used to harass foreigners. As was discussed in chapter 2, cumulation rules permit investigators when determining injury in AD or CVD cases to consider the total effect of all dumped or subsidized imports of a good, instead of just the imports from a single foreign source. Hence, even though the goods from one source may be negligible, cumulation can still lead to an adverse finding for exporters. As was the case with a low de minimis, cumulation rules can encourage domestic producers to use that unfair trade cases to harass foreigners. Limiting the use of cumulation might decrease such harassment.

The constructed value and best information available WTO rules changes are aimed at limiting practices that many developing countries find reprehensible. As was noted in chapter 3, several Thai respondents felt that these practices are not legitimate investigatory techniques and that they are often employed as coercive devices. The Thais are interested in obtaining WTO limitations relating to the means by which data may be acquired, the sources that may be used, and the calculation procedures that may be employed during AD and CVD investigations.

Finally, the rules regarding sunset reviews should be reexamined. As pointed out in chapter 3, the Thais are interested in a rule that would automatically terminate AD and CVD duties after a specified period of time. Such an approach to sunset reviews has merit. As a fallback position, the Thais might push for a clarification and tightening of the calculation procedures that may be used during sunset reviews, for, as was discussed in chapter 2, on occasion these procedures differ from those employed during the initial investigations. Another change the Thais might seek would involve reducing the time period for sunset reviews from five years to three. Currently, WTO rules require a sunset review within five years of the initial AD or CVD determination. A reduction from five years to three would do little harm to domestic American interests, but would have the potential for lessening the impact on developing country exporters.

In addition to the above changes in WTO rules, it is recommended that the WTO agreements on dumping and on subsidies be amended to require that all members must employ a three step process before imposing AD or CVD duties. The first step would determine whether dumping or subsidies are involved in a particular commercial exchange, as is done at present. The second step would require that a hearing be held before AD or CVD duties are imposed. This hearing would give domestic industries affected by the duties a chance to make statements regarding any adverse consequences that might result from the duties. Currently, many countries (including the

United States) do not provide affected parties with an opportunity to inform governmental officials of the harm they may suffer from AD or CVD duties. As a result, the decision to impose AD and CVD penalties is often skewed in favor of those seeking the duties.

The final step would require that a country's chief executive review and approve all decisions about the imposition of AD and CVD duties. As was noted in chapter 2, many countries currently have such a requirement in their AD and CVD laws. The United States does not.[4] Setting up a chief executive review requirement might place yet another restraint on the use of AD and CVD duties by making it less probable that all positive determinations would result in the actual levying of duties. Such a reduction in the number of duties levied could be expected because a chief executive would be likely to consider the broader national interest (which would be discussed in the hearing in step two) before agreeing to take action. Developing countries such as Thailand would have little to lose from provisions requiring a hearing and an executive review since at present in many countries (including the United States) the imposition of duties is nearly automatic if a determination is positive, and they would have something to gain since in at least some cases the decision might be made to forgo duties.

Before concluding this section, another point should be made. This concerns the negotiating tactics that Thailand and other developing countries employ regarding the changes they seek in WTO AD and CVD rules. As Carolyn Rhodes discusses in detail, international negotiations in the context of the GATT and the WTO are based on reciprocity.[5] Under this system, bargaining involves a process of give and take in which no WTO member is expected to make more concessions than other members. In order to obtain something it wants, a member must be prepared to offer other negotiating parties something they want.

In the current context, this means that if Thailand and other developing countries wish to obtain changes in WTO AD and CVD rules, then they must be prepared to offer concessions that are of interest to members, such as the United States, that may not favor those alterations. Possible concessions might relate to issues that many Americans regard as important, such as protection for intellectual property rights, freer trade in services, statements regarding worker's rights, or environmental regulations.[6]

By agreeing to American demands in some of these areas, developing countries might not only induce American representatives to go along with AD and CVD rules changes, but might also increase the probability that Congress would approve the final product of the WTO talks. Final Congressional approval would be more likely because Americans benefiting from the concessions on intellectual property rights or other issues might pressure Congress to take favorable action. This pressure for favorable action might serve as a counterweight to pressure from those who oppose the final WTO deal because they dislike the AD and CVD rules changes. In the absence of such developing country concessions, a counterweight of this sort sort might not exist, and Congressional approval could be problematic. Therefore, developing countries might benefit from making concessions as a bargaining tactic.

International Development

In addition to policy recommendations, this research has broader implications for international development. These implications take three forms. One pertains to the exercise of power in the contemporary international system. The second relates to protectionism, and the third has to do with the interdependence that exists among international actors in today's globalized international arena.

Power in International Relations

Beginning with power, the work herein clearly shows that attempts to influence others and to conduct the international business needed to promote economic growth increasingly are tied to one's ability to devise and/or decipher the numerous complex and arcane rules and procedures that govern the trade relations among international actors.[7] Whereas in the past international influence often was a product of the use of force or the threat to engage in violence, at present many of the most important international power interactions are built on the knowledge one has of legal procedures and rules.

The interview results relating to Thai reactions to American and WTO rules regarding AD and CVD cases clearly illustrate the value of information, for both corporate executives and government officials stated repeatedly that a deficiency in knowledge about American AD and CVD laws was a key problem that left them at a disadvantage when attempting to penetrate the United States market. In part, this disadvantage in knowledge meant that Thai firms might make mistakes that would leave them vulnerable to unfair trade complaints from American corporations. Beyond this, the Thais also indicated that they felt ill prepared for handling the complexities associated with AD and CVD cases and stated that this lost them business.

In effect, in an information age one finds that the ability to understand the law and the way the law is applied can constitute a substantial source of power. At the same time, one also can acquire power by devising regulations that others find it difficult to understand. By using this technique, one can construct formidable legal obstacles to prevent international competitors from gaining ground in one's home market. Clearly, many United States special interests and some members of Congress have learned this lesson, as was illustrated in chapter 2 where the examination of the evolution of American AD and CVD laws showed that these regulations have become extremely difficult to understand for any but the most carefully trained analysts.

An additional thought regarding the exercise of power has to do with what Stephen Krasner labels "meta power" and other researchers refer to as "structural power."[8] Meta power involves a situation in which an actor seeks to dominate others by creating international rules that work to that actor's advantage. Structural power relates to a similar situation in which actors seek to control others by setting up international institutions and other regularized patterns of behavior that work to their advantage.

One result that emerged from this research was the feeling among Thai respondents that future WTO negotiations regarding dumping and subsidies rules will be of crucial importance because they believe that new WTO rules can free them from some of the burdens associated with AD and CVD investigations as they currently are conducted. It was clear that the Thais regard WTO talks as a "high stakes" issue and as the best chance developing countries have for redressing the current AD and CVD environment, which generally is seen as favoring advanced countries. That is, the Thais see WTO negotiations as an opportunity to exercise the meta power that can change a crucial international structure (WTO AD and CVD rules) to their advantage. From the Thai point of view, the problem is how they can overcome their inherent weaknesses as a relatively small and poor country with a limited knowledge base and a dearth of unfair trade specialists.

As was found, the Thais are not without resources and ingenuity as they seek to affect the restructuring of WTO regulations. For one thing, the Thais are cooperating to lead the way toward a new form of international alliance. The Friends of Antidumping is the latest in a series of coalition building exercises by small and developing countries that are designed to promote favorable international outcomes. The Cairns Group during the Uruguay Round of GATT negotiations was an earlier effort of this sort. Another bargaining device the Thais are seeking to employ to their advantage is the effort to link trade to national security. In both cases, one can see that the techniques for exercising power during international trade talks are becoming more sophisticated and are beginning to resemble the types of tactics typically associated with old-fashioned balance of power politics.

Another point should be made regarding the exercise of power in an information age. As has been mentioned several times during this analysis, the

Thais perceive themselves as weak when compared to more advanced countries because Thailand does not have the same pool of specialized trade experts that more advanced societies possess. While this lack of experienced officials can be a handicap in an era in which negotiations affecting trillions of dollars in trade may hinge on relatively obscure and technical international rules changes, it need not be devastating in its effects. This is because the Thais can turn to foreign advisers such as the trade attorneys they work with in the United States. As was mentioned in chapter 3, the Thais uniformly believed that the American lawyers they hire do a good job handling their cases and advising and even training them. Hence, although the Thais may feel disadvantaged when it comes to expertise, this absence of an important power resource in the world of trade does not carry the same deleterious implications as may have been the case in past international systems because it is increasingly possible to redress such shortages through international acquisitions of talent. Indeed, this acquisition often may come from the very society of the government that is posing the problems one seeks to surmount, as happens when Thai firms hire Washington attorneys to help them overturn trade decisions. In other words, while advantages in obtaining and understanding information may be of growing importance in exercising power in at least some contexts, it is possible in today's global arena to partially erase that advantage by purchasing what one needs from a foreign source. It is also possible to employ the domestic resources of another country to one's own ends and to use them to oppose that country's government.

Protectionism
The second implication of this research for international development pertains to protectionism. As was mentioned in chapter 1, at present one of the most widely accepted strategies for promoting economic growth and development calls for developing societies to export to advanced country markets. This approach, however, frequently runs into opposition from those in wealthy societies who compete with developing country exports. When this opposition arises, the natural result is calls for protectionist policies that bar or limit imports from the developing world.

In the past, the technique used to grant protection to domestic producers was the tariff. As was noted in chapter 2, in the years since World War II, in the United States and in other advanced societies tariffs have been lowered consistently. This has meant that American producers who fear international competition have been forced to seek other forms of protection. One avenue that Congress has made available for these American businesses is the duties associated with the penalties applied to unfair trade. In an effort to make these duties more readily accessible, Congress has expanded the definition of unfair trade and has broadened the reach of AD and CVD regulations on several occasions in recent years.

While these expanded definitions have allowed more American corporations to obtain relief, they also have opened up a new means for obtaining protection. This new protection relates to using antidumping and countervailing duty cases to harass one's foreign competitors. Here, the goal often is not the imposition of duties that might increase foreign prices to a level that would make imports unattractive to American consumers. Instead, the goal of the new protectionism frequently is to embroil foreign competitors in time consuming unfair trade investigations that cost so much in legal fees that the foreigners are harmed even if they win their case. Moreover, when foreign competitors are under the cloud of an unfair trade investigation, there is always the possibility that American customers will change their purchases to favor American made goods.

The new protectionism means that the analysis of obstacles to trade must become more sophisticated. The mere examination of tariffs and non-tariff barriers no longer is sufficient. Instead, one must look closely at the nuances of the rules that are created to govern trade. Regulations that might appear harmless, such as de minimis rules, may have considerable potential for hampering trade when they are in the hands of a creative mind looking to block imports. Thus, one finds that legal rules and procedures take on a new level of political importance. To a degree, this means that when studying trade, political scientists must return to the roots of their discipline that were built on the study of institutional regulations and processes for it is only through a complete understanding of institutional rules and procedures that one can grasp the nature of the new protectionism.

The new protectionism also implies that foreigners wishing to do business in the United States and in other advanced societies must develop a high degree of expertise not only in their product lines, but that they must also have a thorough understanding of the political institutions and of the rules and procedures found in other societies. Either that, or they must have the money to hire experts who can guide them through the often overwhelmingly complex world of political and legal processes. In itself, the need for such expertise can serve as a substantial impediment to doing business abroad.

Thus, the new protectionism is built on foundations that are much more difficult to assault than was the case with the protective tariff. First, as was discussed in chapter 1, many of the arguments in favor of this protectionism are based on the notion that one faces a contest between right and wrong in which foreigners are using unscrupulous practices to penetrate a market. The concept of unfair trade is predicated on the idea that the behavior in question violates basic principles of propriety. As a result, negotiations to lower these types of trade barriers can become emotional as proponents maintain that the barriers are needed to ensure a level international trade playing field while opponents point to the use of the barriers as little more than a device for harassing foreigners. Under these circumstances, analysts interested in international development would best serve their cause by trying to sidestep emotion by focusing on such arcane and technical issues as de minimis levels, cumulation rules, and constructed value procedures. In addition, it might prove valuable to tie unfair trade talks to larger foreign policy interests and to concessions regarding other trade issues, as was mentioned above.

The second foundation that makes the new protection extremely troublesome is the highly technical nature of the rules and procedures that guide the actions taken. As has been illustrated repeatedly herein, AD and CVD legislation has become so complex that it can require a sophisticated analyst to untwist the many nuances involved in the typical case. Hence, this protection takes on a subtlety that renders it hard to fight, both because the mere filing of a case may mean victory if the foreigner is unable to respond appropriately and because international talks to rein in this type of protection can easily become bogged down in obscure issues.

The result of the above is that developing governments and corporations face an ever more difficult task as they seek to do business in advanced markets. Not only do they confront the emotions associated with "unfair" trade, but they also face the task of acquiring the expertise essential to defending their interests. These problems promise to make negotiations to eliminate barriers to trade lengthier and more contentious as time passes.

International Interdependence
The third implication of this analysis for development has to do with interdependence. Interdependence is defined as a situation in which two or more international actors develop a mutual reliance upon one another. Within the context of this reliance, however, it is assumed that all actors retain their autonomy and are able to attempt to protect their self-interests.[9] Much of the work pertaining to international interdependence has examined such things as how asymmetries in interdependent relationships can confer advantages on one partner as opposed to others, how economic sanctions can be used to exercise power, and on how interdependence leads to the spread of cultural, ideological, and political values. The work from this research indicates that international interdependence has reached a point where, as was noted above, it has become important for foreigners to become familiar with the in-

tricacies of the legal systems and regulations of other societies. This is true both for foreign governments and for foreign corporations, and is especially true for actors from the developing world. Actors from across the globe already face many problems that only can be solved if one understands the legal environment in other countries. These problems promise to multiply in the future.

Another implication for interdependence is found in the growing role the GATT and the WTO have played since World War II as referees in the international game of commerce. Because of the influence of the GATT and the WTO and because most actors see international commerce as promising the possibility of enormous gains, interdependence in the world of trade increasingly takes place in an arena that is unlike that found in other issue areas. While anarchy continues to play a major role in most of the other types of interactions found in international politics, the commercial world is rapidly developing structures that limit the degree to which anarchical behavior can take place. Evidence of this is found in the discussion in chapter 2 of how American unfair trade rules have been altered to conform to GATT and WTO requirements. It is also found in chapter 3, where Thai respondents indicated their interest in using the WTO to soften American AD and CVD regulations. As international actors, both advanced and developing, seek to expand their foreign commercial contacts one can expect more international regulations and structures that will further bind countries to common codes of conduct and reduce the effects of anarchy in the trading arena.

In addition, this research says something about the dependence that poor countries experience within an interdependence relationship. Many international analysts maintain that the structure of the international system favors advanced countries at the expense of developing countries. According to this view, the operation of the international arena is so tilted against developing societies that they find it extremely difficult to promote economic growth and to behave autonomously. As a result, the poor remain poor, while rich societies prosper and become wealthier. Within this environment, it is argued that there are few options available for developing countries that wish to employ an international strategy that relies on trade to create economic development.

When one considers the results from the interviews in chapter 3, one might at first conclude that Thailand is overly dependent on the United States and might be affected as described above. In particular, one might think of the disparities between the United States and Thailand when it comes to the role each country plays in world trade, the fact that Thailand accounts for a small proportion of American trade while the United States is responsible for a large share of Thai trade, and the degree to which the Thais rely on foreign attorneys for knowledge and training about American trade laws and to represent their interests. These factors seem to point to a dependence built in part on the ability to dominate through the use of complex and difficult to understand legal procedures and rules. In effect, in this type of dependence, rules are used to promote advanced country interests and to block poorer societies from benefiting from international commerce. Development by poor countries is obstructed because the poor are unable to gain access to the export markets they need if they are to grow and prosper.

This picture, however, does not tell the whole story. As was just noted, those focusing on the detrimental effects of dependence depict developing countries as unable to use international structures to their own benefit because these structures work in the interests of advanced countries. Nonetheless, the Thai respondents in chapter 3 did not appear to see things this way, expressing the belief that the WTO dispute settlement system could be used to redress their grievances. Indeed, the Thais pointed to several cases in which the WTO has given assistance to developing countries. The Byrd Amendment case is an example. The Thais also indicated that they expect current and future WTO negotiations to yield results that will work to their advantage as far as AD and CVD regulations are concerned. In other words, the Thais regard an important international structure, the WTO, as a source of assistance and opportunity.

Moreover, the Thais stated that they had confidence in the American appeals system as a means for getting a fair hearing when they lose the first round in a trade case in the United States. This also flies in the face of dependence arguments for it indicates that legal processes in an advanced country can be used to the advantage of a poor society. Finally, the assertion that dependence robs a country of its independence of action is contradicted by the Thai participation in international coalitions, such as the Friends of Antidumping, to push for changes in international regulations and by the Thai efforts to protect their interests through lobbying activities in Washington. Each of these activities indicates that while dependence in the contemporary world does include restrictions, it offers opportunities as well. Hence, while American-Thai relations might be asymmetrical, there are reasons to believe that they do not overly restrict the Thai ability to use international commerce to further Thai interests.

In closing, it should be noted that the findings herein indicate the need for additional research. In particular, it is important for future work to explore in detail the difficulties that the world's least developed countries confront as they seek to employ trade to promote economic growth and development. It is vital to identify these problems so that international structures and practices can be created to facilitate the economic progress of these poor societies both to help stamp out the misery that plagues many of their people and to eliminate one of the most potent sources of international instability.

Notes

1. Research on interest group lobbying with regard to trade has a long tradition. Among the very first works to examine the subject was the classic E. E. Schattschneider, *Politics, Pressures, and the Tariff*, New York: Prentice-Hall, 1935. Another important work is Raymond A. Bauer, Ithiel de Sola Pool, and Lewis Anthony Dexter, *American Business and Public Policy*, New York: Atherton Press, 1964. A more recent treatment of the subject can be found in I. M Destler, *American Trade Politics*, Washington, DC: Institute for International Economics, 1995.

2. See Judith Goldstein, *Ideas, Interests, and American Trade Policy*, Ithaca, N.Y. Cornell University Press, 1993, pp. 197-205 and Judith Goldstein, "Ideas, Institutions, and American Trade Policy," *International Organization*, vol. 42, no. 1, Winter 1988, pp. 179-217.

3. For a discussion of American trade policy before World War II, see Wayne S. Cole, *Roosevelt and the Isolationists, 1932–1945*, Lincoln: University of Nebraska Press, 1983; Robert Dalleck, *Roosevelt and American Foreign Policy, 1932–1945*, New York: Oxford University Press, 1979; Robert Divine, *The Illusion of Neutrality*, Chicago: University of Chicago Press, 1962; and William L. Langer and S. Everett Gleason, *The Challenge of Isolation, 1937–1940*, New York: Council on Foreign Relations, 1952. Discussion of trade during the Cold War can be found in Burton I. Kaufman, *Trade and Aid: Eisenhower's Foreign Economic Policy, 1953–1961*, Baltimore: Johns Hopkins University Press, 1982; John M Rothgeb, Jr., *U.S. Trade Policy: Balancing Economic Dreams and Political Realities*, Washington, DC: 2001, chaps. 5, 6, 8 and Steve Dryden, *Trade Warriors: USTR and the American Crusade for Free Trade*, New York: Oxford University Press, 1995.

4. For a discussion of the role of the president in American unfair trade cases, see Goldstein, *Ideas, Interest, and American Trade Policy*, chap. 5.

5. Carolyn Rhodes, *Reciprocity, U.S. Trade Policy, and the GATT Regime*, Ithaca, N.Y. Cornell University Press, 1993.

6. For a discussion of the American interest in these issues, see Rothgeb, *U.S. Trade Policy*, pp. 236-38.

7. The reader is reminded that in chapter 1 power was defined as controlling the behavior of others when they do not wish to be controlled. For a discussion of how international relations scholars define power, see John M Rothgeb, Jr., *Defining Power: Influence and Force in the Contemporary International System*, New York: St. Martin's Press, 1993, chap. 2.

8. Stephen Krasner, "Transforming International Regimes: What the Third World Wants and Why," *International Studies Quarterly*, vol. 25, no. 1, March 1981, p. 122;

Davis Bobrow, Steve Chan, and Simon Reich, "Trade, Power, and APEC: Hirschman Revisited," *International Interactions*, vol. 24, no. 3, 1998, pp. 190-92.

9. One of the earliest and best discussions of interdependence is found in James A. Caporaso, "Dependence, Dependency, and Power in the Global System: A Structural and Bahavioral Analysis," *International Organization*, vol. 32, no. 1, Winter 1978, pp. 13-43. Another excellent presentation is in Robert Keohane and Joseph S. Nye, J., *Power and Interdependence*, third edition, New York: Longman, 2001. For discussions of asymmetrical interdependence, see Michael Dolan, Brian Tomlin, Harold Von Riekhoff, and Maureen A. Mot, "Asymmetrical Dyads and Foreign Policy: Canada-U.S. Relations, 1963-1972," *Journal of Conflict Resolution*, vol. 26, no. 3, September 1982, pp. 387-422 and John M Rothgeb, J., *Foreign Investment and Political Conflict in Developing Countries*, Westport, CT, Praeger, 1996.

Glossary of Terminology and Abbreviations

AD (antidumping duty): A penalty tariff assessed against goods that are sold in an export market at less than fair value. The duty is designed to raise the price of the good to the fair value price.

Annual Reviews: A requirement introduced into American law in 1979 that all dumping and countervailing duty decisions be reevaluated yearly in order to ensure that penalty tariffs are maintained at the proper level and that suspension agreements (see below) are properly enforced.

Antidumping Act of 1921: Law that established the modern approach to combating foreign dumping in the United States. Set antidumping fees as the means for handling dumping, eliminated the need to establish predatory intent on the part of foreigners, made decisions regarding the imposition of duties administrative, and permitted the use of constructed values for determining less than fair value.

BIA (Best Information Available): An information gathering procedure that the International Trade Administration of the Commerce Department may use when foreign producers and/or governments do not cooperate by providing information during unfair trade investigations. On occasion, the information obtained with this procedure may come from the American firms that filed the unfair trade complaint.

BMTN (Thai Bureau of Multilateral Trade Negotiations): An agency within the Thai Mistry of Commerce, the BMN is responsible for developing Thai negotiating positions at the WTO and in other international trade bargaining sessions. This agency also monitors the WTO dispute settlement system and plays a role in resolving bilateral disputes about AD and CVD actions.

BOI (Thai Board of Investment): Housed in the Office of the Prime M̵ister, the BOI encourages domestic and foreign investment, promotes economic growth and development, and assists Thai firms facing foreign CVD actions.

BOT (Bank of Thailand): An independent Thai government agency that funds the Thai Export-Import Bank, promotes research and development, manages the Thai banking system, and assists Thai firms facing foreign CVD actions.

Bounty: A payment a government gives to its exporters. Also referred to as a subsidy.

BTIR (Thai Bureau of Trade Interests and Remedies): An agency in the Thai M̵istry of Commerce, the BTIR helps conduct Thai AD and CVD investigations, analyzes foreign AD and CVD regulations, examines the effects on the Thai economy of foreign AD and CVD actions, and assists Thai corporations with foreign AD and CVD complaints.

Byrd Amendment: Named for Democratic Senator Robert Byrd of West Virginia and passed by Congress in 2000, this law is formally known as the Continued Dumping and Subsidy Act. It requires that the proceeds from collecting AD and CVD duties be paid to the American producers affected by the foreign dumping and/or subsidies. Several WTO members brought the law before a WTO dispute resolution panel, claiming that it violated WTO rules. In 2002 the panel ruled that the law does infringe on WTO rules, but the matter remains unresolved.

Circumvention: Involves a circumstance in which foreign producers seek to side-step American AD and /or CVD rules by shipping slightly altered or updated products or by sending the goods to a third country for final assembly.

Constructed Values: A procedure used to calculate dumping margins when the sales in the exporting market are negligible. The constructed value involves adding the estimated cost of production, packing charges, transportation costs, and an appropriate profit margin.

Cumulation: A procedure employed during the injury phase of AD and CVD investigations wherein the International Trade Commission examines the effects on American producers of all of the dumped or subsidized imports of a particular good instead of basing the injury determination on a case by case basis.

CVD (countervailing duty): A penalty tariff assessed against exports that receive a subsidy from the government of their country of origin. The duty is designed to eliminate any pricing advantage that results from the subsidy.

De minimis: The dumping or subsidy margin that terminates an American AD or CVD investigation. If an investigation reveals that the margin is below the de minimis, then no further action is taken.

DOC (United States Department of Commerce): Cabinet-level organization that handles many of the trade problems that confront the United States. Includes within its structure the International Trade Administration (see below).

Domestic Subsidy: Introduced in 1988 legislation, a domestic subsidy is any benefit provided by a government to its producers that lowers production costs, even if obtaining the benefit does not depend on the recipient's export performance. An example is reduced utility rates for industrial users.

Dumping: Term applied to a situation in which foreign producers offer products for sale in export markets at prices that are less than fair value in an attempt to gain an abnormally large share of the market.

FTI (Federation of Thai Industries): An umbrella private sector organization of twenty-eight private industry clubs in Thailand. Channels information about the private sector to the government, advises individual companies about AD and CVD complaints, and analyzes the effects foreign AD and CVD actions have on Thai businesses.

GATT (General Agreement on Tariffs and Trade): Set of rules and procedures set up in 1947-1948 to regulate both negotiations to lower trade barriers and international commercial exchanges.

Injury Test: A requirement in American trade law that AD and/or CVD duties only can be imposed if the foreign unfair trade practices damage American producers. The International Trade Commission conducts the investigation to determine whether an injury has occurred.

ITA (International Trade Administration): An agency within the United States Commerce Department that handles unfair trade investigations. Determines whether dumping and/or subsidies exist, what the dumping and/or subsidy cost advantages (also referred to as margins) are, and sets the level of any duties that will be imposed.

ITC (International Trade Commission): The name given to the Tariff Commission when it was renamed in 1974. An independent United States government agency, the ITC conducts trade investigations and holds hearings to determine when protection should be granted to American producers. Handles injury investigations in unfair trade cases.

Joint WTO Committee (Joint WTO Committee on Commerce, Industry, and Banking in Thailand): Includes as members the Thai Board of Trade, the Federation of Thai Industries, and the Thai Bankers'Association. The Joint WTO Committee helps the Thai government develop negotiating positions in WTO talks, assists the private sector as it deals with a more open Thai economy, and transmits information to the government from the private sector.

Kennedy Round: General Agreement on Tariffs and Trade (GATT) negotiations held during the 1960s. Named for President John F. Kennedy.

LTFV (Less Than Fair Value): A standard for determining when foreign-made goods are dumped. LTFV may be determined in any of three ways: (1) by comparing the price in the country of origin to the price in the United States, (2) by comparing the price in other export markets to the price in the United States, or (3) by comparing a constructed price to the price in the United States. In each case, if the comparison price is higher than the price in the United States, the good is considered as being sold at LTFV.

MOC (Thai Ministry of Commerce): The cabinet-level agency in the Thai government that handles trade-related issues, including all AD and CVD problems.

Negative Dumping Margin: When a dumping investigation reveals that the price in a foreign market is lower than the price in the United States. In effect, this is the opposite of dumping.

Non-dutiable Imports: Goods that are not subject to a tariff when they enter the United States.

OTCA (Omnibus Trade and Competitiveness Act of 1988): A major American trade law that among other things addressed the problems of circumvention and third-country dumping.

Positive Dumping Margin: When a dumping investigation reveals that the price in a foreign market is higher than the price in the United States, indicating that dumping exists.

Predatory Pricing: A part of a strategy for harming competing businesses in which a corporation charges lower prices in some markets than are charged in others. The goal is to capture market share from competitors in the market where the low price is charged.

RTAA (Reciprocal Trade Agreements Act of 1934): A law passed in 1934 that allows the president to lower tariffs by negotiating mutual reductions with other countries. Many analysts regard this law as the cornerstone of the modern American approach to trade policy.

Special and Differential Treatment: Privileges that the World Trade Organization grants to its developing country members that allows them to observe standards that are not as stringent as the standards for advanced countries.

Specificity: One of the standards the World Trade Organization uses for differentiating between allowable and unacceptable subsidies. Specificity refers to whether a subsidy is available for use by everyone in a society (an example is publicly financed roads) or just by those who produce goods for export. If the subsidy is just for those who export, it is specific and is not allowable.

Subsidies: Payments provided by a foreign government to its exporters to allow them to sell their goods in foreign markets at abnormally low prices.

Sunset Review: A requirement found in the Uruguay Round Agreements Act of 1994 that a review be conducted within five years of the initial imposition of AD and/or CVD duties to determine whether the dumping or subsidies continue to exist. If the dumping and/or subsidies have stopped, then the AD and/or CVD duties are halted.

Suspension Agreements: An arrangement wherein foreigners are able to avoid AD and/or CVD duties by raising their prices to a level that eliminates any advantage gained from dumping and/or subsidies.

Tariff Commission: United States government agency created in 1882 to investigate the trade practices of other countries and to provide advice to the president and Congress. Also handled the determination of injury in unfair trade cases. Its name was changed to the International Trade Commission in 1974.

TFPA (Thai Food Processors' Association): An industry club for Thai food packing and trading firms. Promotes information exchanges among its members, helps with foreign AD and CVD cases, helps secure legal assistance for member companies, and transmits complaints about foreign AD and CVD actions to the Thai government.

Third Country Dumping: A practice wherein a foreign producer dumps goods in another country thereby denying American producers an export market.

TISIC (Thai Iron and Steel Industry Club): An industry club for Thai firms in the iron and steel industry. Helps Thai firms facing foreign AD and CVD complaints and brings industry complaints to the attention of the Thai government.

Tokyo Round: GATT negotiations held during the 1970s.

TPPG (Thai Pineapple Packers' Group): The front line organization that handles the trade problems confronting its member corporations. Assists pineapple packing companies with foreign AD actions.

Traffic Light Approach: The method used by the World Trade Organization to differentiate between subsidies that are forbidden at all times (red light subsidies), subsidies that are questionable (yellow light subsidies), and those that are permissible (green light subsidies).

Undertaking: An action specified in a suspension agreement (see above) whereby foreigners avoid AD or CVD duties by raising the price of their products to a level that eliminates the advantages gained by dumping or by receiving a subsidy.

Unfair Trade: A situation in which a foreign producer or its government manipulates market conditions to its advantage and to the detriment of businesses in export markets.

Upstream Subsidy: A payment from a government or customs union that reduces the cost of a good that is used to make another product that is subject to a countervailing duty. An example is bicycles made with subsidized steel.

URAA (Uruguay Round Agreements Act of 1994): The legislation that wrote into American law the outcomes associated with the Uruguay Round of GATT negotiations.

Uruguay Round: GATT negotiations held in the late 1980s and early 1990s. Led to the establishment of the World Trade Organization.

USTR (United States Trade Representative): Cabinet-level official in the executive branch who conducts United States trade negotiations and advises the president on trade policy.

WTO (World Trade Organization): International organization established in 1995 that regulates trade among its members through the creation and maintenance of rules and procedures that facilitate commercial activity.

Zeroing: A controversial practice wherein negative dumping margins (see above) are set to zero when making the calculations in dumping investigations. This practice makes it easier to reach a positive dumping determination when the investigation involves averaging prices over a period of time.

APPENDIX B

~

Questions for the Thai Dumping and Subsidy Survey

I. Procedural Questions

a. Do the Thais feel comfortable with United States AD and CVD procedures?

b. Does the United States give adequate prior public notice of AD investigations as required under Article 12 of the WTO Antidumping Agreement?

c. Do the Thais feel they are given an adequate opportunity for input when the United States conducts AD and CVD investigations?

d. Do United States authorities provide adequate explanations for procedures and details of the cases brought against Thai producers so that the Thais feel they understand the case against them and what is expected of them during the investigation?

e. How well do the Thais understand the time deadlines associated with American AD and CVD cases?

f. Do the Thais understand that the best information available (BIA) will be used if proper information is not provided during an investigation?

g. Do the Thais realize that BIA can be obtained from United States complainants during an investigation?

h. Do the Thais understand the procedures the United States uses during on-the-spot investigations in Thailand? Do the Thais feel that these procedures affect Thai interests negatively?

    i. Do the Thais feel that United States procedures are sufficiently transparent so that all parties to AD and CVD cases understand what is going on?

    j. How do the Thais feel about the United States law passed in 2000 (the Byrd Amendment) that diverts AD and CVD duties from the United States Treasury to the American companies that are the complainants in a case?

        i. Do the Thais consider this diversion of funds an illegal subsidy to United States companies under WTO subsidy rules?

        ii. Do the Thais feel that the issues raised by this law have been handled properly by the WTO dispute settlement system?

        iii. Do the Thais plan to seek negotiations about this law during future WTO negotiations?

    k. Do the Thais feel that the United States conforms with WTO AD and CVD rules?

    l. Does the United States provide Thailand with the special treatment that developing countries are required to receive under WTO AD and CVD rules?

    m. Does the United States adhere to applicable WTO rules when determining the size of any AD and CVD duties?

    n. Does the United States adhere to the traffic light approach set up under WTO rules for handling subsidies?

II. Knowledge Questions

    a. Knowledge of United States Law

        i. Does the Thai government feel that it has a sufficient staff of trained specialists who understand American AD and CVD laws?

        ii. Is the Thai government forced to rely on experts it hires in the United States to handle its AD and CVD cases?

        iii. Does the Thai government feel comfortable in relying so heavily on American legal experts to assist it with AD and CVD cases?

        iv. Does the Thai government feel that it should place a high priority on training Thai scholars and professionals so that it would have a group of Thais with expertise in American trade policy?

        v. Do Thai corporations have staffs of trained specialists who understand United States AD and CVD laws?

        vi. Do Thai corporations place a priority on hiring specialists who understand United States AD and CVD laws?

        vii. Does the United States government provide any assistance to the Thai government or to Thai corporations to help them understand United States AD and CVD laws?

viii. Does the WTO provide any assistance in understanding United States AD and CVD laws?

b. Knowledge of WTO Rules

   i. Does the Thai government feel that it has a sufficient staff of trained experts who understand WTO AD and CVD rules?

     1. If not, then who does the Thai government rely on for assistance with its WTO AD and CVD cases?

     2. Does the Thai government feel comfortable relying on this source for assistance?

     3. Does the Thai government feel that it should place a priority on training Thai scholars and professionals so that they could handle Thai AD and CVD cases before the WTO?

   ii. Do Thai corporations have sufficient staffs of trained experts to help them understand WTO AD and CVD rules?

     1. If not, then who do Thai corporations rely on for assistance with their WTO AD and CVD cases?

     2. Do Thai corporations feel comfortable relying on this source for assistance?

     3. Do Thai corporations feel that they should place a priority on training their employees to understand WTO AD and CVD rules?

   iii. Do the Thais feel the WTO provides sufficient assistance to help countries understand WTO AD and CVD rules?

   iv. Do the Thais cooperate with other countries to gain assistance in understanding WTO AD and CVD rules? If so, which countries?

III. Assistance Questions

a. How much assistance does the Thai government provide to Thai companies in understanding United States and WTO AD and CVD rules?

b. Does the Thai government conduct seminars and other training sessions to inform Thai firms about United States AD and CVD rules?

c. Does the Thai government provide written material, such as booklets, that explain United States AD and CVD rules?

d. Does the Thai government assist Thai corporations in their search for legal assistance in the United States when the corporations face American AD cases?

e. Does the Thai government help Thai firms fill out the forms involved in United States AD cases?

f. Does the Thai government defray any of the costs Thai corporations confront when dealing with United States AD cases?

IV. Burden Questions

    a. Are the costs associated with United States AD and CVD complaints unduly burdensome for the Thai government or for Thai corporations? What are these costs?

    b. How much does it cost to hire attorneys in the United States to handle Thai AD and CVD cases?

    c. Does the mere initiation of a United States AD or CVD case hinder the ability of Thai firms to continue doing business in the United States?

    d. Do importers in the United States shy away from doing business with Thai corporations that are the subject of American AD or CVD investigations or actions?

    e. Do the Thais feel that American companies use the filing of AD and CVD cases to harass their Thai competitors?

    f. Have American companies altered the way they pursue CVD cases in light of the traffic light approach found in WTO rules?

    g. Do the Thais feel that United States AD and CVD laws are designed to discourage foreign firms from doing business in the United States?

    h. Do the Thais feel that the Byrd Amendment encourages American corporations to file unfair trade cases so that they can receive the payments provided for under the law?

    i. Do the Thais feel that United States firms use the filing of AD and/or CVD cases to keep foreign competitors out of the American market? If so, have the Thais been able to use the WTO to obtain redress for such behavior?

V. Settlement Questions

    a. Does the filing of a dumping complaint in the United States incline Thai corporations to consider restricting their exports in exchange for the termination of the complaint?

    b. What role does the Thai government play in any process that involves restricting exports in exchange for the termination of an American dumping complaint?

    c. Do the Thais feel that American complainants are aiming for deals that restrict Thai exports when they file AD complaints?

    d. Do the Thais feel that the WTO plays a role in informally resolving unfair trade cases? If so, what is that role?

    e. Under WTO guidelines, a complaint relating to subsidies can be handled either by taking a case to the WTO dispute settlement system or by conducting a domestic investigation and imposing a CVD. Which approach do the Thais prefer to use for handling their subsidized imports? Which procedure does the United States most often use with its imports from Thailand? Why do the Thais prefer one approach over the other? Why do the Thais believe the United States employs one approach instead of the other? Are some cases handled one way, while others are handled another way? Why is this the case?

f. When faced with a negative finding in a foreign subsidy investigation, which way do the Thais prefer to respond:
   i. Voluntarily raise the price for the good to offset the value of the subsidy;
   ii. Volunteer to terminate the subsidy; or
   iii. Accept the imposition of a CVD by the foreign government.
   iv. Why do the Thais prefer one of the above approaches to the others?

g. Has the passage of the Byrd Amendment affected the solution the Thais prefer for American subsidy cases (see the preceding question)?

h. Do the Thais continue to experience "gray area" (for example, VER) demands from the United States as proposed solutions for AD and/or CVD cases even though WTO rules forbid such deals? Do the Thais prefer gray area deals as a means for resolving unfair trade cases? If so, why?

VI. Retaliatory Questions
   a. Does the Thai government impose retaliatory dumping judgments against American companies when the United States imposes AD duties against Thai corporations? If not, why not?
   b. Do United States dumping or subsidy investigations or actions incline the Thai government to consider taking positions at the WTO or in any other international forum that are opposed by the United States?

VII. Appeal Questions
   a. Do the Thais appeal adverse United States AD and CVD decisions to the appropriate American authorities?
   b. Do the Thais have confidence in the American appeals process?
   c. Do the Thais appeal adverse United States AD and CVD decisions to the WTO?
   d. Do the Thais have confidence in the WTO dispute settlement system?
   e. Do the Thais feel they have a reasonable chance of winning a WTO case against the United States?
   f. Do the Thais feel that the WTO dispute settlement system is biased against certain types of countries? If so, which countries?

g. Do the Thais feel that filing an appeal (either with United States authorities or with the WTO) will lead to retaliation by the United States?

VIII. Cooperation Questions

a. Does the Thai government willingly supply appropriate data during United States AD and/or CVD investigations? If not, why not?

b. Do Thai corporations willingly supply appropriate data during United States AD and/or CVD investigations? If not, why not?

c. Does the Thai government encourage Thai firms to cooperate with the United States government when it conducts AD and CVD investigations?

d. What types of problems impede the ability of Thai corporations to cooperate with the United States government during its AD and CVD investigations?

e. What types of problems impede the ability of the Thai government to cooperate with the United States government during its AD and CVD investigations?

IX. Negotiations Questions

a. Do the Thais feel that they had sufficient input into the Uruguay Round negotiations that created the WTO Antidumping and Subsidies and Countervailing Duty Agreements?

b. What role did Thailand play in the AD and CVD negotiations during the Uruguay Round?

c. Do the Thais feel that the current WTO AD and CVD rules are adequate or do they feel that further negotiations are in order?

d. Do the Thais plan to play a vigorous role in future WTO AD and CVD talks?

e. What issues do the Thais plan to raise in future WTO AD and CVD negotiations?

f. Do the Thais feel that they are at a disadvantage when negotiating about WTO AD and CVD rules? Why are they at a disadvantage?

g. Do the Thais feel that current WTO AD and CVD rules favor some WTO members over others? Which ones and why?

h. Did Thailand cooperate with any other countries when negotiating about AD and CVD rules during the Uruguay Round?

i. Is Thailand cooperating with other countries when negotiating about AD and CVD rules during the Doha Round? If so, which countries and why?

j. Do the Thais feel that cooperating with other countries during WTO AD and CVD talks has produced benefits for Thailand? If so, describe the benefits.

k. Do the Thais feel that some countries have been able to dominate WTO and /or GATT AD and CVD negotiations? If so, which countries? Have the same countries dominated negotiations consistently?

X. Impact Questions

    a. Do United States AD and CVD investigations and/or negative determinations create any of the following problems in Thailand:

        i. Political or economic instability due to lost jobs or revenue?

        ii. Problems relating to the maintenance of economic growth? If so, are these problems localized, or are they more widespread?

        iii. Problems leading to bankruptcy for Thai firms?

        iv. Problems for any Thai companies that do business with the Thai firms affected by United States AD or CVD rulings?

    b. Does the Thai government help Thai firms find new international markets when they are adversely affected by United States AD or CVD rulings?

    c. Does the Thai government provide any other form of assistance to Thai firms that are adversely affected by United States AD and CVD rulings?

    d. Does the Thai government terminate subsidies to Thai firms when it receives a complaint from the United States? If so, how do Thai companies react to these terminations?

    e. Does Thailand cooperate with other countries when they are jointly named in a United States AD or CVD case? If so, is this cooperation useful? What forms does the cooperation take?

    f. Does the Thai government provide assistance to Thai communities that are affected by adverse United States AD or CVD rulings? If so, what forms does this assistance take?

    g. Does the Thai government provide special training programs for workers who lose jobs due to adverse AD or CVD rulings?

Index

About the Authors

John M. Rothgeb, Jr., is Professor of Political Science and Distinguished Scholar of the Graduate School at Miami University in Oxford, Ohio. His research interests include U.S. trade policy, the politics of development, international theory, and American foreign policy. Professor Rothgeb is the author of four books, including *U.S. Trade Policy, Foreign Investment and Political Conflict in Developing Countries, Defining Power,* and *Myths and Realities of Foreign Investment in Poor Countries.* Professor Rothgeb also has published numerous articles in such journals as *Journal of Politics, International Studies Quarterly, Journal of Conflict Resolution, Western Political Quarterly, Journal of Peace Research, World Development,* and *Comparative Political Studies.*

Benjamas Chinapandhu is Assistant Professor of Political Science at Ramkhamhaeng University in Bangkok, Thailand. Professor Chinapandhu earned her Ph.D. at Miami University in Oxford, Ohio. Her research interests include U.S. trade policy, EU trade policy, and issues relating to the World Trade Organization. Professor Chinapandhu is the author of articles appearing in *Political Science Review* and *Southeast Current.*